Come Celebrate!

A Hymnal Supplement

Betty Pulkingham
Mimi Farra
Kevin Hackett
Editors

Pew Edition

Cathedral
MUSIC PRESS

Celebration

Folio © 1990 Mel Bay Publications, Inc., Pacific, MO 63069, U.S.A.

1 2 3 4 5 6 7 8 9 0

Acknowledgement

Many people have contributed to the preparation of this supplement. Appreciation is expressed to Ruth Wieting for overall assistance; to Marian Holmes and Wiley Beveridge for proofreading; to Erba Ritter and Bob Morris for preparation of the indices; and to all the members of the Community of Celebration for their prayers, patience, and support throughout this endeavor. Finally, we owe a debt of gratitude to Ros Brown whose gifts of precision and musicianship in the preparation of the final manuscript brought this book into being.

Betty Pulkingham
Mimi Farra
Kevin Hackett
Editors

TABLE OF CONTENTS

Table of Contents, continued

Foreword

The Spirit of God has dramatically renewed the Church in the past few decades. All over the world, God's people have been drawn together in an exciting new way, as vibrant living cells of the Body of Christ. And is in corporate worship that we witness the work of renewal across the spectrum of differing Christian traditions. New language and new music, renewed life in ancient traditions, and a reclaimed understanding of the Church as the community of the New Covenant all attest to the real presence of the life of God in the world today, in and through the Church. In worship, the people of God are nurtured and empowered and equipped to be disciples of Jesus Christ, to celebrate the Good News.

Celebration is the mark of the life of Jesus' disciples, individually and corporately. Celebrating our new life in Christ, celebrating our new life as a people called from the land of oppression and death to a new way of living, is the means by which the world around us is drawn to the saving knowledge of God.

Celebrating all of life, "the whole of it," has been a hallmark of the Community of Celebration's life for over 15 years. **Come Celebrate!** represents the fruit of our life of worship. Its contents are eclectic: international, intergenerational, and sacramental, reflecting our life together as the family of God.

Most of the songs and hymns contained herein have their origins in our common life. Many, though credited to a single composer, are genuinely the product of the whole Community. All have proven their usefulness in a variety of settings around the world.

We are proud to offer this collection (designed to supplement The Hymnal 1982) as a resource for enriching parish family worship with simple songs and hymns, on Sundays, at home, at work, and in the dailiness of life.

Performance Notes

Voice

The human voice is the principle musical instrument in Christian worship. It is people who worship God. Instruments may assist, but it is people—men, women, and children who gather to name the Name, to remember the story, to proclaim the Good News—who praise the Lord. That we worship in song is only natural. The marriage of text and tune, offered freely to God, can give voice to the deepest yearnings of the soul for union with the Other.

Congregational song is one of the most vital elements in Christian worship. It is a means by which an otherwise diverse gathering of people can experience themselves as corporate. Sensitivity to the musical idiom, the occasion of worship, and those standing or sitting near-by is essential in the production of a blended corporate sound. It is the task of those responsible for worship leadership to convey such concepts to the people they serve, both by instruction and example.

Vocal harmonies are provided on many songs in this collection to encourage part-singing. Several rounds, canons, and two- and three-part songs are included as well. Descants are provided for many songs; they should be used with care, best sung by a few light voices, only, as an enhancement to the original melody. Alternatively, descant parts can be played by a solo instrument, e.g., flute or violin.

Vocal Leadership

Vigorous congregational or group singing depends on some form of vocal leadership. Choirs have traditionally fulfilled this function, but in a growing number of congregations, who may or may not have a choir, the ministry of a cantor or song-leader is one of growing importance. The purpose of this type of leadership—usually visible—is to encourage and inspire the people's praise, and it is made all the more effective if it is supported and under-girded by the choir. The function of the cantor or song-leader must never be seen as one of performance.

Many of the songs in this collection are designed to be improvisational. They are cast in folk-song form and, as such, depend on the active participation, spontaneity, and creativity of the gathered community, responding to the mood of the moment, the event in progress. Leadership must exercise pastoral care and wisdom in order to incorporate and channel these elements into corporate worship.

Sound Reinforcement

The sensitive use of sound reinforcement is a practical necessity in larger settings. Each element (voice, guitar, piano) that is amplified should be done so to reinforce its natural acoustic properties, never to dominate or create an electronic sound.

The equipment required for successful reinforcement of music is different from that which is normally used for the spoken word. A qualified sound technician with musical training can provide advice and direction in assessing the needs of specific spaces.

Organ

While many of the songs in this collection are ideally suited to piano accompaniment, most can be successfully rendered on the organ with modest reduction. The letter of the guitar chord represents the pedal note, providing a 'figured bass' of sorts (see notes for Bass). The melody is played by the right hand (solo stops may be utilized on many songs), while the left hand fills out the rest of the chord. Light registrations will yield a more pleasing result.

Piano

In a growing number of churches, whether by choice or necessity, the piano provides the principal accompaniment for worship. In smaller settings (parish halls, chapels, church schools, home gatherings), it is even more common.

Accompanying group singing requires a strong but musical tone. Sensitive use of the pedal will "enlarge" the sound and assist in phrasing.

The accompaniments provided in this collection were written with the player of modest abilities in mind. Generally speaking, the melody should dominate during the introduction and first-singing of a song's principal theme(s). After it is firmly established, however, improvisation can be encouraged (though the integrity of the musical idiom should be maintained).

Bass

A bass instrument (electric bass guitar, string bass, or 'cello) can add a solid "foundation" to an instrumental ensemble, as well as strengthening the rhythmic pulse. Root position is generally preferred, though inversions occasionally appear, notated as follows:

> (guitar chord) A/C# (bass note)

In this instance, the bass plays the note following the stroke. As a rule, "less is more." Bass walks

> (guitar chord) C/C...B...A (bass notes)

may be used sparingly. Elaborate bass "licks" should be avoided. The purpose is to undergird the singing of the people, not to perform.

Percussion

The selective use of hand-held percussion instruments can enhance the inherent rhythmic qualities of many songs in this collection. Simple parts for tambourine, triangle, claves, maracas, bongos, and finger cymbals can be played by ordinary people with minimum rehearsal. Handclaps and fingersnaps should not be overlooked as a percussion effect as they also provide a means for physical involvement in worship. Handclaps should be light and rhythmic, using three or four fingers against the opposite palm. Heavy-handed clapping quickly becomes monotonous, is apt to accelerate tempo, and can be unmusical.

"Less is more" is a good guideline for using percussion. Consider playing the tambourine only on a refrain, for instance, and, even them, waiting until the song is firmly established before coming in. Avoid complicated rolls and patterns; simple motifs are much more effective. Add additional instruments as the song progresses, building to the "climax" of the final refrain(s) or verse.

Other instruments

The addition of orchestral or band instruments to an ensemble can enrich the worship experience. Use these instruments to introduce the melody, reinforce unison singing, provide descants and obligatos, and add tonal texture and color. Inexperienced players may need specific parts written out.

Virtually any combination of instruments can work, but care must be taken to utilize the unique qualities of each, taking into account the players' proficiency, other instruments in the ensemble (two trumpets might be too much in some situations, while a trumpet and a flute would be workable, for instance), and the musical idiom (flute rather than trumpet or 'cello, for instance, would provide more suitable accompaniment to C-188 Allelu).

Players need not be professional (using the volunteer resources at hand is highly commendable and desirable). They do need an understanding of and commitment to the discipline of corporate worship and to the discipline of rehearsal and study for their instrument.

Guitar

In recent years, the use of the guitar in corporate worship has had checkered success: its presence has not always been an enhancement to the occasion of worship. The problem, however, has usually more to do with the insensitive use of the instrument than the instrument itself. The player's lack of skill and/or rehearsal, the inability to be heard, and repertoire inappropriate to the setting or event are commonly cited grievances. Any of these factors can foster misunderstanding or prejudice against a genre of sacred song that has long been part of the Christian tradition.

Just as a good organist or pianist will employ specific techniques to lead congregational singing, so must the guitarist. Playing for one's own enjoyment is different from leading singing around a campfire which is different still from playing in the context of liturgical worship. The same song might be used in each scenario, but it will necessarily be played differently in order to be effective.

As a portable instrument, the guitar is ideally suited for gatherings where a keyboard is not available (picnics, home gatherings, chapels, church schools, etc.), but using it to lead worship implies an understanding of its rhythmic qualities, a thorough knowledge of common chord tablature, and a basic sensitivity to tempo, rhythm, and musical idiom.

A twelve-string guitar is most suitable for use in public worship. The employment of octave strings reinforces its natural volume, as well as creating the instrument's characteristic "ring." A six-string steel-string instrument would be the next choice. A nylon string guitar will probably be effective only for solo accompaniment or in very small gatherings.

Service Music

C-101

Venite

The verses of this invitatory psalm may be sung by a cantor or choir.

Words: Book of Common Prayer
Music: Betty Carr Pulkingham

Jubilate Deo

(O Praise the Lord)

C-102

This rhythmic setting of Psalm 100 may be sung unaccompanied.

Words: Psalm 100, adapted, Stephen Ball
Music: Stephen Ball

C-103

Jubilate Deo
(O Be Joyful in the Lord)

Refrain

Brightly

O _____ be joy-ful in the Lord! _ O be joy-ful in the

Lord! Let us make a joy-ful noise, let the whole earth re - joice! _____

_____ O be joy-ful in the Lord, all ye lands! _____

Verse 1

1. Know that the Lord, he is God: _____ he has

made us, we are his. _____ We are the sheep of his

to Refrain

pas - ture, _____ the peo - ple of his hand. _____

Verse 2

2. En - ter his gates with thanks - giv - ing: _____

come in-to his courts with praise. _____ Be thank - ful un - to

to Refrain

him, _____ and speak good of his Name. _____

Verse 3

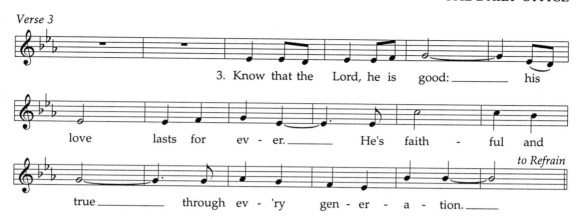

3. Know that the Lord, he is good: _____ his love lasts for ev - er. _____ He's faith - ful and true _____ through ev - 'ry gen - er - a - tion. _____

to Refrain

The refrain of this song is enhanced by the use of hand-held percussion instruments: tambourine, claves, maracas, etc.

Words: Psalm 100, adapted, Jonathan Asprey
Music: Jonathan Asprey

C-104

O Gracious Light
(Phos Hilaron)

This modal setting could be accompanied with guitar and flute.

Words: Book of Common Prayer
Music: Sandy Hardyman Stayner

Psalm 134

(Come and Bless the Lord)

C-105

Come and ___ bless the Lord, all you who serve him, who stand night ___
af-ter night in the house of the Lord. ___ Lift up your hands in the sanc-tua-ry
and bless the Lord. The Lord, the mak-er of heav'n and earth, bless you from
Zi-on; the Lord, the mak-er of heav'n and earth, bless you from Zi-on.

This setting of Psalm 134 is especially appropriate at Compline.

Words: Psalm 134
Music: Graeme Wise
Copyright © 1975 ST. PAUL'S OURTREACH TRUST, NEW ZEALAND. All rights reserved.

C-106

The Grace

This setting of the Grace may be sung unaccompanied.

Words: 2 Corinthians 13:14, adapted
Music: St. Aidan's Community

Lord, Have Mercy

(Kyrie, 3-fold)

Words: Book of Common Prayer
Music: *King of Glory Mass*, Betty Carr Pulkingham

C-108

Kyrie Eleison

The refrain of this "troped" Kyrie may be used without the verses.

Holy God
(Trisagion)

C-109

Ho - ly God, Ho - ly and Might - y, Ho - ly Im -
mor - tal One, Have mer - cy up - on us.

May be sung three times in succession.

Words: Book of Common Prayer
Music: *El Shaddai Setting for Holy Communion*, Betty Carr Pulkingham

C-110   # Holy, Holy, Holy Lord
(Sanctus)

Words: Book of Common Prayer
Music: *King of Glory Mass*, Betty Carr Pulkingham

Holy, Holy, Holy Lord
(Sanctus)

C-111

With rich sonority

Ho - ly, ho - ly, ho - ly Lord, God of pow-er and might, hea-ven and earth are full of your glo-ry. Ho - san - na in the high - est. Bless - ed is he who comes in the name of the Lord. Ho - san - na in the high - est.

Words: Book of Common Prayer
Music: *El Shaddai Setting for Holy Communion*, Betty Carr Pulkingham

Christ Has Died

C-112

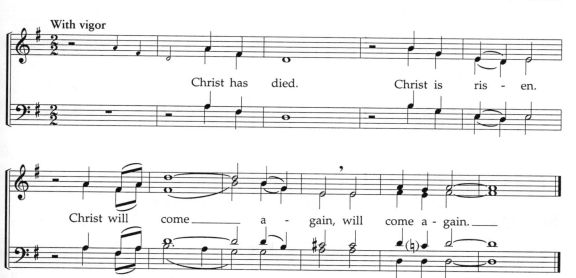

With vigor

Christ has died. Christ is ris - en. Christ will come a - gain, will come a - gain.

Words: Book of Common Prayer
Music: *King of Glory Mass*, Betty Carr Pulkingham

C-113   Christ Has Died

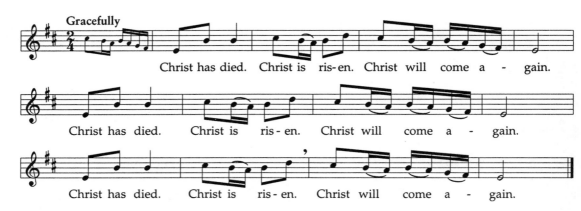

Christ has died. Christ is ris-en. Christ will come a - gain.

Christ has died. Christ is ris-en. Christ will come a - gain.

Christ has died. Christ is ris-en. Christ will come a - gain.

Words: Book of Common Prayer
Music: *El Shaddai Setting for Holy Communion*, Betty Carr Pulkingham

C-114   The Lord's Prayer

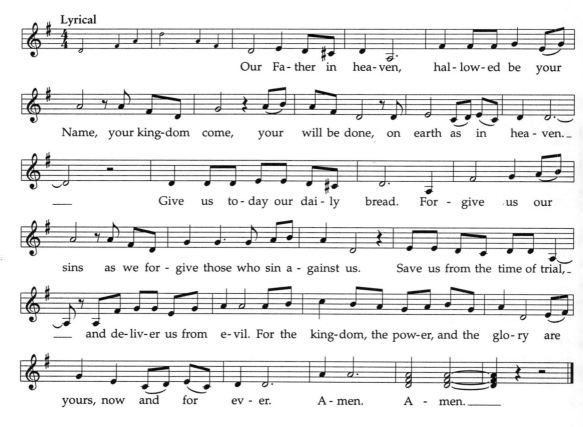

Our Fa-ther in hea-ven, hal-low-ed be your

Name, your king-dom come, your will be done, on earth as in hea-ven.

Give us to-day our dai-ly bread. For - give us our

sins as we for-give those who sin a - gainst us. Save us from the time of trial,

and de-liv-er us from e-vil. For the king-dom, the pow-er, and the glo-ry are

yours, now and for ev - er. A - men. A - men.

Words: Book of Common Prayer
Music: *King of Glory Mass*, Betty Carr Pulkingham

The Lord's Prayer

Our Father in heaven, hallowed be your Name,

your king-dom come, your will be done, on earth as in

heaven. Give us to-day our dai-ly bread.

freely
Forgive us our sins as we forgive those who sin a-gainst us.

Save us from the time of tri-al, and de-liv-er us from

e-vil. For the king-dom, the pow-er, and the

slowly
glo-ry are yours, now and for ev-er. A-men.

Words: Book of Common Prayer
Music: *El Shaddai Setting for Holy Communion*, Betty Carr Pulkingham

Lamb of God

(Agnus Dei)

Lamb of God, you take a-way the sins of the

world: have mer-cy on us. Lamb of God, you take a-way the

sins of the world: grant us peace.

Words: Book of Common Prayer
Music: *El Shaddai Setting for Holy Communion*, Betty Carr Pulkingham

C-117

Jesus, Lamb of God
(Agnus Dei)

Je - sus, Lamb of God: have mer - cy on us.

Je - sus, bear-er of our sins: have mer - cy on us.

Je - sus, re - deem-er of the world: give us your

peace, _____ give us your peace. _____

Je - sus, Lamb of God: have mer - cy on us. Je - sus,

(Basses hum or sing ooh) -

bear-er of our sins: have mer - cy on us. Je - sus, re-

- *(Basses sing text)*

deem-er of the world: give us your peace, _____

Optional descant

give us your peace.___ Je - sus, have mer - cy

give us your peace.___ Je - sus, Lamb of God: have mer - cy

on us. Je - sus, have mer - cy on us.

on us. Je - sus, bear-er of our sins: have mer - cy on us.

rit. e dim.

Je - sus, give us your peace._____

rit. e dim.

Je - sus, re - deem-er of the world: give us your peace._____

Words: Book of Common Prayer
Music: *King of Glory Mass*, Betty Carr Pulkingham

C-118 The Song of Moses

This song is especially suitable for use during Easter.

Words: Exodus 15:1-15, 21, adapted, Betty Carr Pulkingham
Music: Betty Carr Pulkingham

C-119 The Song of Simeon
(Nunc Dimittis)

Words: Luke 2:29-32
Music: *Port Arthur*, Mimi Farra

Blessing and Honor

This song is a suitable alternative setting of A Song to the Lamb.

Words: Adapted from Revelation 4 & 5 by Jodi Page-Clark and Kevin R. Hackett
Music: *Appalachia*, Jodi Page-Clark and Kevin R. Hackett
Copyright © 1975, 1988 CELEBRATION. All rights reserved.

C-121

Great and Wonderful

This song is a suitable alternative setting of The Song of the Redeemed.

Words: Revelation 15:3-4, adapted, Wiley Beveridge
Music: Wiley Beveridge

Glory to God
(Gloria in Excelsis)

Words: Book of Common Prayer
Music: *King of Glory Mass*, Betty Carr Pulkingham

Songs and Hymns

C-123   Good Morning, This Is the Day

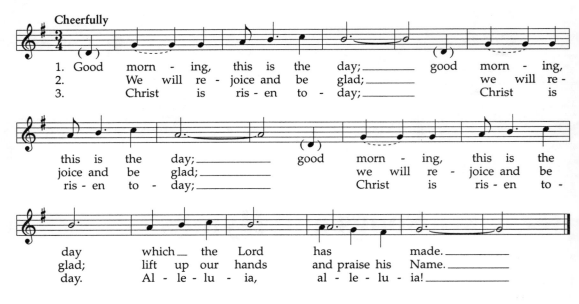

Cheerfully

1. Good morn - ing, this is the day;_____ good morn - ing,
2. We will re - joice and be glad;_____ we will re -
3. Christ is ris - en to - day;_____ Christ is

this is the day;_____ good morn - ing, this is the
joice and be glad;_____ we will re - joice and be
ris - en to - day;_____ Christ is ris - en to -

day which__ the Lord has made._____
glad; lift up our hands and praise his Name._____
day. Al - le - lu - ia, al - le - lu - ia!_____

Words and Music: David McKeithen

Morning Psalm

With simplicity

1. How beau-ti-ful the morn-ing and the day; my
2. How glo-ri-ous the morn-ing and the day; my
3. How boun-ti-ful the bless-ings that he brings of
4. How mer-ci-ful the work-ings of his grace, a-
5. How bar-ren was my life be-fore he came sup-

1. heart a-bounds with mu-sic, my lips can on-ly
2. heart is still and lis-tens; my soul be-gins to
3. peace and joy and rap-ture that make my spi-rit
4. rous-ing faith and ac-tion my soul would nev-er
5. ply-ing love and heal-ing; I live now to ac-

1. say: how beau-ti-ful the morn-ing and the day.
2. pray to him who is the glo-ry of the day.
3. sing: how boun-ti-ful the bless-ings that he brings.
4. face with-out his match-less mer-cy and his grace.
5. claim the maj-es-ty and won-der of his Name.

Words: Owen Barker
Music: *St. Owen*, Sherrell Barker Prebble

C-125 The Steadfast Love of the Lord

Suitable for use in the Burial Office.

Words: Lamentations 3:22-26, 31-33, 40-41, adapted, Edith McNeill
Music: Edith McNeill

Alleluia, He Is Coming

This song is useful during Easter. Simple hand actions can be devised to portray the text.

Words and Music: Martha Butler

C-127   Lord, Hear Our Prayer

Words and Music: William Bay

C-128   My Lord, He Is A-comin' Soon

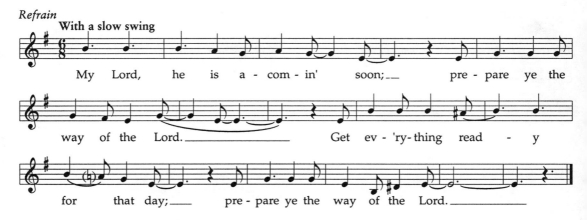

Verse 1

1. If you're a - sleep, it's time to wake up;___ a - wake, O sleep-er, a - rise._____ If you're in the dark, it's time to be lit;___ ___ a - wake, O sleep-er, a - rise!_____

to Refrain

Verse 2

2. Come, Lord Je - sus, come in - to my heart;___ pre - pare ye the way of the King._____ He is com-ing, he's com-ing soon;_ ___ pre - pare the way of the King!_____

to Refrain

Verse 3

3. John the Bap - tist now calls to us:___ "Re - pent and change your ways._____ The true Mes - si - ah is com - ing soon._ ___ He is the hope of the world!"_____

to Refrain

Use fingersnaps on the off-beat to capture the "blues" flavor of this song.

Words: Laura Winnen
Music: Jeff Cothran

C-129

On Jordan's Bank

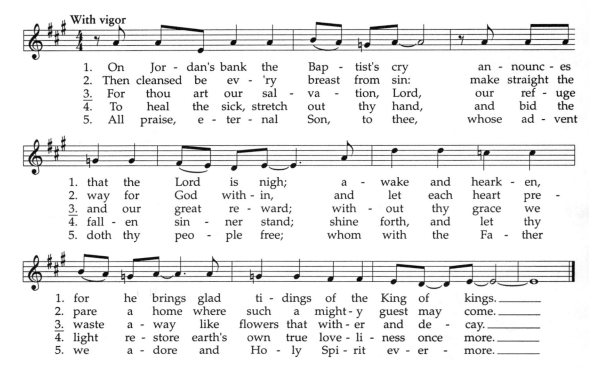

With vigor

1. On Jordan's bank the Baptist's cry announces
2. Then cleansed be ev - 'ry breast from sin: make straight the
3. For thou art our sal - va - tion, Lord, our ref - uge
4. To heal the sick, stretch out thy hand, and bid the
5. All praise, e - ter - nal Son, to thee, whose ad - vent

1. that the Lord is nigh; a - wake and heark - en,
2. way for God with - in, and let each heart pre -
3. and our great re - ward; with - out thy grace we
4. fall - en sin - ner stand; shine forth, and let thy
5. doth thy peo - ple free; whom with the Fa - ther

1. for he brings glad ti - dings of the King of kings.____
2. pare a home where such a might - y guest may come.____
3. waste a - way like flowers that with - er and de - cay.____
4. light re - store earth's own true love - li - ness once more.____
5. we a - dore and Ho - ly Spi - rit ev - er - more.____

Words: Charles Coffin, alt.
Music: *St. John the Baptist*, Gary Miles
Copyright © 1974, 1975 CELEBRATION. All rights reserved.

Christmas Gloria

C-130

(two, three, or four-part round)

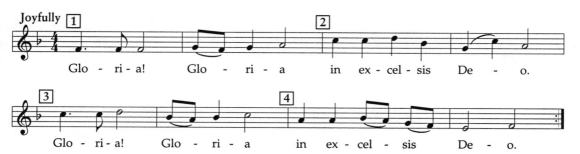

Random ringing of small bells enhances this song.

Words: trad.
Music: Kevin R. Hackett

C-131

Christmas Lullaby

Verses
Gently rocking

1. Cra - dle rock - ing, cat - tle low - ing, bright star guid - ing
2. Moth - er Ma - ry, watch - ing care - fully by the light of
3. Who could guess, to see you lie there, that you come to
4. Do you know, so weak and help - less, of the grace you

us to see lit - tle Christ - child in the man - ger;
one bright star, bread of hea - ven, soft - ly sleep - ing,
bring a sword? Prince of Peace up - on the man - ger,
bear to us? Do you dream yet of the king - dom

light of all the world to be.
gen - tle gift of God to us.
with a price up - on your soul.
you will one day bring to pass?

Refrain

Hal - le - lu - jah, ho - ly child. Ho - san - na in the high - est.

Glo - ri - a, Em - man - u - el. Ho - san - na in the high - est.____

Words and Music: Jodi Page-Clark

The Light of Christ
(two-part song)

Refrain **With simplicity**

Part I

The light of Christ has come in-to the world. The

Part II

The light of Christ has come in - to the world.

light of Christ has come in-to the world.

The light of Christ has come.

Verse 1

1. We must all be born a-gain to see the king-dom of God; the

to Refrain

wa-ter and the Spi-rit bring new life in God's love.

Verse 2

2. God gave up his on-ly Son out of love for the world, so that

to Refrain

all who be-lieve in him will live for - ev - er.

Verse 3

3. The light of God has come to us so that we might have sal - va-tion; from the

to Refrain

dark-ness of our sins we walk in-to glo - ry with Christ Je - sus.

This two-part song may be sung antiphonally between men and women.

C-133 Fear Not, for I Have Redeemed You

Refrain
With assurance

Fear not, for I have re-deemed _____ you; I have called you by name. I have called you by name; _____ you are mine. _____

Verse 1

1. When you pass through the wa-ters I will be with you; _____ and through riv-ers, they will not o-ver-whelm you. _____ When you walk through the fire you will not be burned; _ the flames will not con-sume you. _____

Verse 2

2. Be-cause you are pre-cious and I love you, _____ you whom I

formed for my glo-ry,_____ you whom I called by my

Name,_____ I will gath-er to-geth-er._____ *to Refrain*

Verse 3

3. You are my wit-ness-es; I have cho-sen you_____ that you may

know and be-lieve me._____ You are my ser-vants for the

world to see._____ I am the Lord, I'm a-mong you._____ *to Refrain*

Verse 4

4. It's time now to lay a-side the for-mer things;_____ a new day has

dawned, do you see it?_____ I'm mak-ing a way in the

wil-der-ness,_____ and riv-ers to flow in the des-ert._____ *to Refrain*

Verse 5

5. The riv-ers that flow in the des-ert_____ give drink to

my cho-sen peo-ple;_____ to quench their thirst and to

strength-en them,_____ that they might show forth my praise._____ *to Refrain*

Verses of this "Gospel song" can be sung by a soloist, or by men and women, alternately.

Words: Isaiah 43:1-21, adapted, Jodi Page-Clark
Music: *Allen*, Jodi Page-Clark

C-134

I Will Rejoice

Other verses may be added: "I will sing to the Lord..." "I will trust in the Lord..." "I will delight in the Lord..."

Words: Habakkuk 3:17, Job 13:15
Music: Jan Harrington

Lord, Who Throughout These Forty Days C-135

This contemporary setting of the traditional Lenten hymn utilizes the first stanza as a refrain. Verses may be sung by a soloist or choir, or by men and women, alternately.

Words: Claudia Hernaman, alt.
Music: *St. David's Radnor*, Betty Carr Pulkingham

C-136

Turn Me, O God

Refrain **Thoughtfully**

Turn me, O God, _____ and I shall be turned. _____

Verse 1

1. Though I wan-der through des - o - la - tion _____ I will find you there. Though the wa-ters o'er - whelm my soul, e - ven so you are Lord. _____

to Refrain

Verse 2

2. Cre - ate in me a new heart. _____ I would see your face. Take not your Ho - ly Spi - rit from me, I would see your face. _____

to Refrain

Verse 3

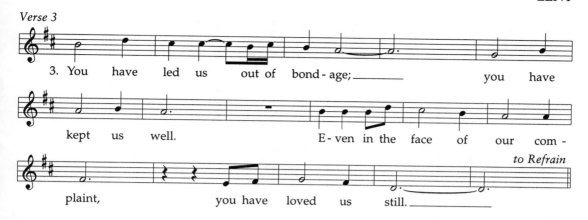

3. You have led us out of bond-age; ___ you have

kept us well. E-ven in the face of our com-

to Refrain

plaint, you have loved us still. ___

For themes of corporate repentance, the refrain of this song could be sung, "Turn us, O God."

Words and Music: Jodi Page-Clark

Worthy the Lamb

C-137

(two or three-part round)

Wor - thy the Lamb who was slain for us.

Wor - thy, wor - thy the Lamb. ___

Other verses may be added: "Mighty the Lamb..." "Holy the Lamb..." "Jesus the Lamb..."
This song is appropriate during Communion.

Words and Music: Richard Gillard

C-138   **Canticle of the King**

Refrain
Majestically

Now the King of Glo-ry is come to sup with us:
break out the sil-ver and crys-tal and wine, for the King of Glo-ry will
dine this day with us, and he will feed us for all time.___

Verse 1

1. Cast be - fore him palms and ban - ners: Je - sus the Mas - ter
comes as our King. Shout ho - san-nas, pro - claim him Lord:
to Refrain
Je - sus the Sa - vior is com - ing.___

Verse 2

2. Sing ho - san-nas loud - er and strong - er: Je - sus the Mas - ter
pass - es your way. Praise him and bless him, Cal - va-ry's Lamb:
to Refrain
soon he will bear your sins a - way.___

Verse 3

3. Hon - or and glo - ry, praise with-out ceas - ing be - long to Christ, the
Mas - ter and King. Songs full of won - der, songs full of praise:

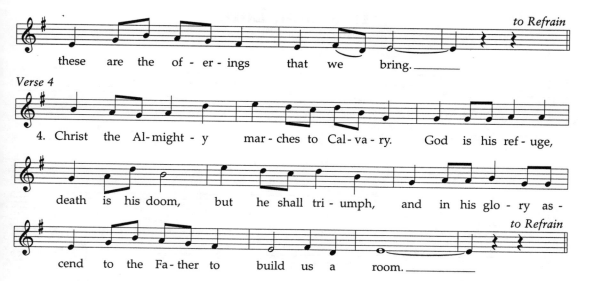

to Refrain

these are the of-er-ings that we bring._____

Verse 4

4. Christ the Al-might-y mar-ches to Cal-va-ry. God is his ref-uge,

death is his doom, but he shall tri-umph, and in his glo-ry as-

to Refrain

cend to the Fa-ther to build us a room._____

This song is particularly useful as an offertory; verses may be sung by a soloist or choir, with everyone joining on the refrain.

Words and Music: Tom Beckwith

C-139

Hosanna, Lord!

Refrain **Brightly**

We cry, "Ho - san - na, Lord," yes, "Ho - san - na, Lord," yes, "Ho - *Optional tenor descant*

Ho - san - na! Ho - san - na!

san - na, Lord," to you. We cry, "Ho - san - na, Lord," yes, "Ho -

Ho - san - na to you. Ho - san - na!

san - na, Lord," yes, "Ho - san - na, Lord," to you.

Ho - san - na! Ho - san - na to you.

Verse 1

1. Be - hold, our Sa - vior comes. Be - hold the Son of our God. He
to Refrain
of - fers him - self, and he comes a - mong us, a low - ly ser - vant to all.

Verse 2

2. Chil - dren wave their palms as the King of all kings rides by. Should
to Refrain
we for - get to praise our God, the ve - ry stones would sing.

Verse 3

3. He comes to set us free. He gives us lib - er - ty. His

to Refrain

vic- t'ry o - ver death   is the e - ter - nal sign of God's   love   for   us.

Children of all ages will enjoy waving their "palms" (the palms of their hands) as verse 2 is sung. This song is especially suitable on Palm Sunday.

Words: Mimi Farra
Music: *Luton*, Mimi Farra

C-140   Jesus, Remember Me

This response may be sung repeatedly as a "chant". It is especially appropriate on Good Friday.

Words and Music: Jacques Berthier

Sanna

"Sanna" is an abbreviation of the word, "hosanna". Sung at a stately tempo, this song is useful in a solemn procession, sung unaccompanied.

Words: trad.
Music: anon., arr. Betty Carr Pulkingham
Arr. © 1975 CELEBRATION. All rights reserved.

C-142 The Foot Washing Song

Verses of this song are scored in a "Gelineau-style" chant and are best sung by a soloist or small group of singers. The refrain is easily sung by all.

Words: John 13, adapted, Shirley Lewis Brown
Music: Shirley Lewis Brown

Christ the Lord Is Risen!

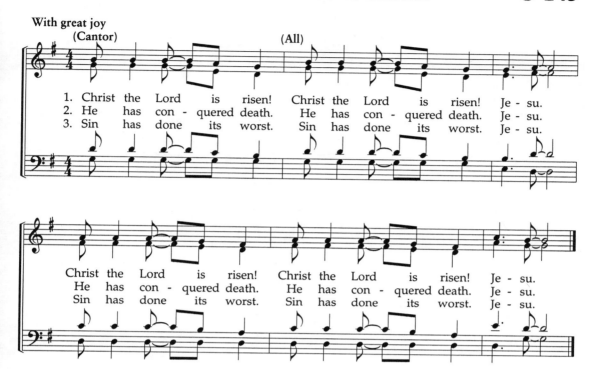

4. He is King of kings. He is King of kings. Jesu.
5. He is Lord of lords. He is Lord of lords. Jesu.
6. All the world is his. All the world is his. Jesu.
7. Come and worship him. Come and worship him. Jesu.
8. Christ our Lord is risen! Christ our Lord is risen! Jesu.
9. Hallelujah! Hallelujah! Jesu.

This African Easter hymn may be sung accompanied by only percussion instruments: conga drums, bongos, claves, maracas, tambourine, and hand claps. The "Hallelujah's" may be repeated ad lib.

Words: Tom Colvin
Music: *Garu*, Ghanaian folk song, arr. Kevin R. Hackett

C-144

Hallelujah Today!

With a medium rock beat

1. Christ the Lord is ris-en to-day!
2. Love's re-deem-ing work is done;
3. Lives a-gain our glo-rious King;
4. Soar we now where Christ has led,

An-gel hosts and mor-tals say,
fought the fight, the bat-tle won;
where, O death, is now your sting?
fol-low-ing our ex-alt-ed Head.

} Hal-le-lu-jah! Hal-le-lu-jah! Hal-le-lu-jah to-day!

Raise your joys and tri-umphs high; sing, you heav'ns and
Death in vain for-bids him rise; Christ has o-pened
Once he died our souls to save, where is your vic-to-
Made like him, like him we rise, ours the cross, the

This contemporary setting of the traditional Easter hymn has particular appeal to youth. A drum set would be an excellent addition to the accompanying instrumental ensemble.

Words: Charles Wesley, alt.
Music: *Potter's Green*, Betty Carr Pulkingham
Copyright © 1974, 1975 CELEBRATION. All rights reserved.

C-145

¡Resucitó!

"Resucitó" is Spanish for "He arose." It is pronounced, "Ray-soo-see-toh".

Words: Kiko Argüello, trans., Susan Abbott
Music: Kiko Argüello
Music and Spanish text Copyright © 1973 EDICIONES MUSICAL PAX. Sole U.S. Agent: OCP PUBLICATIONS.
English text Copyright © 1988 OCP PUBLICATIONS. All rights reserved.

C-146

O Clap Your Hands

(two or three-part round)

(to Part II)

Lord with the sound of the trum - pet.

(to Part III)

God is the King ———— of all the earth.

(to Part I)

Glo - ry be to God on high! ————

This rhythmic setting of verses from Psalm 47 may be sung as a two or three-part round.

Words: Psalm 47:1-2, adapted, Wiley Beveridge and Bill Shehee
Music: Wiley Beveridge
Copyright © 1974, 1982 CELEBRATION. All rights reserved.

C-147

We See the Lord

This simple song portrays the Lord enthroned in majesty. It segues easily with "He is Lord" (following).

Words: Isaiah 6:1-3
Music: anon., arr. Betty Carr Pulkingham

He Is Lord

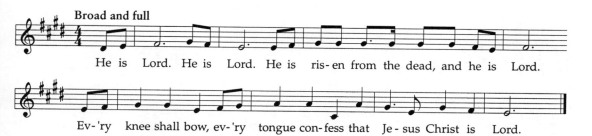

Broad and full

He is Lord. He is Lord. He is ris-en from the dead, and he is Lord.

Ev-'ry knee shall bow, ev-'ry tongue con-fess that Je-sus Christ is Lord.

Words: Philippians 2:9-11
Music: anon.

C-149

Come, Holy Spirit
(two-part song)

This two-part song may be sung antiphonally between men and women.

Words and Music: Mark Foreman

Fear Not, Rejoice and Be Glad

C-150

Refrain

With breadth

Fear not, re-joice and be glad; the Lord has done a great thing, has poured out his Spi-rit on all who live, on those who con-fess his Name.

Verses

1. The fig tree is bud-ding, the vine bear-eth fruit, the
2. We shall eat in plen-ty and be sat-is-fied, the
3. "My peo-ple will know that I am the Lord, their
4. His chil-dren will dwell as a bo-dy of love, a

wheat fields are gold-en with grain. Thrust in the sick-le, the
moun-tains will drip with sweet wine. "My chil-dren shall drink of the
shame I have tak-en a-way. My Spi-rit will lead them to-
light to the world they will be. Life shall come forth from the

to Refrain

har-vest is ripe, the Lord has giv-en us rain.
foun-tain of life, my chil-dren will know they are mine."
geth-er a-gain, my Spi-rit will show them the way."
Fa-ther a-bove, God's word shall set each of us free.

This song celebrates the work of the Holy Spirit in the Body of Christ.

Words: Joel 2:21-24, 26-29, adapted, Priscilla Wright
Music: *Clay*, Priscilla Wright

C-151   **All Saints' Litany**

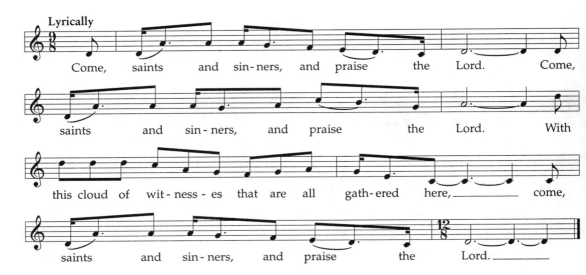

This song provides opportunity to celebrate the lives of all the saints: names of departed loved ones can be used; names of members of the congregation can be used; names of any of the great cloud of witnesses can be used. "Come (name) and (name) and praise the Lord..."

Words: Hebrews 12:1, adapted, Robert J. Stamps
Music: David Stearman

Come to the Waters

C-152

This song is suitable for use at Baptism.

Words and Music: Jodi Page-Clark

C-153   Father, Mother, Keeper, Friend

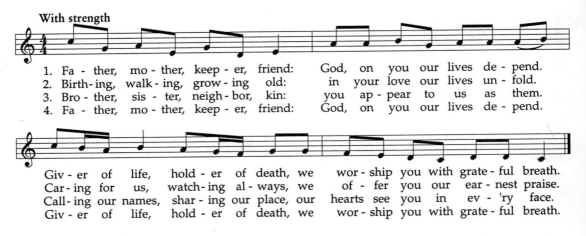

With strength

1. Fa - ther, mo - ther, keep - er, friend: God, on you our lives de - pend.
2. Birth- ing, walk - ing, grow - ing old: in your love our lives un - fold.
3. Bro - ther, sis - ter, neigh - bor, kin: you ap - pear to us as them.
4. Fa - ther, mo - ther, keep - er, friend: God, on you our lives de - pend.

Giv - er of life, hold - er of death, we wor - ship you with grate - ful breath.
Car - ing for us, watch- ing al - ways, we of - fer you our ear - nest praise.
Call- ing our names, shar - ing our place, our hearts see you in ev - 'ry face.
Giv - er of life, hold - er of death, we wor - ship you with grate - ful breath.

This hymn celebrates the risen life of Christ here on earth today.

Words: Teresa Moore, alt.
Music: *God With Us*, Kevin R. Hackett

Forever Loved

C-154

Verses
Tenderly

1. You're called by name, for - ev - er loved, a -
dopt - ed as a child of God. Now one with us, the
fam - i - ly of those who know and love the Lord.

2. Marked as Christ's own, signed by the cross where
Je - sus for our sins once died, with Je - sus bur - ied
in his death, called to con - fess Christ cru - ci - fied.

3. Raised to new life, a life of grace, set
free from sin, in Christ to grow; his res - ur - rec - tion
to pro - claim, his love in all of life to know.

4. Sealed by the Spi - rit, Lord of life, sus -
tained and strength-ened by his might. Joined to the Church to
share, with us, the in - her - i - tance of saints in light.

Refrain
Lord, in your hands we place your own. Lord,
In your hands we place your own. Lord,
Lord, in your hands we place your own. Lord,

in their lives make your love known.

This baptismal hymn addresses words of encouragement to the newly baptized and offers a prayer for their knowledge of God.

Words: Rosalind Brown
Music: *Sara H.*, Kevin R. Hackett

C-155   God Has Called You

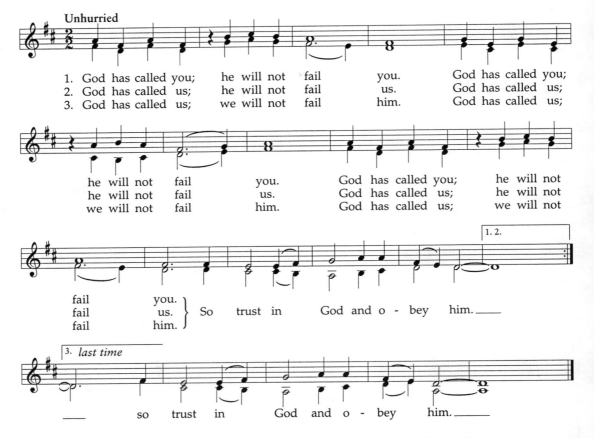

Unhurried

1. God has called you; he will not fail you. God has called you;
2. God has called us; he will not fail us. God has called us;
3. God has called us; we will not fail him. God has called us;

he will not fail you. God has called you; he will not
he will not fail us. God has called us; he will not
we will not fail him. God has called us; we will not

fail you. ⎫
fail us. ⎬ So trust in God and o - bey him. ____
fail him. ⎭

3. last time

____ so trust in God and o - bey him. ____

This song can be personalized by using individual names: "God has called Susan; he will not fail her."

Words and Music: Diane Davis Andrew

God Is Our Father

C-156

C-157   Jesus Is the Rock

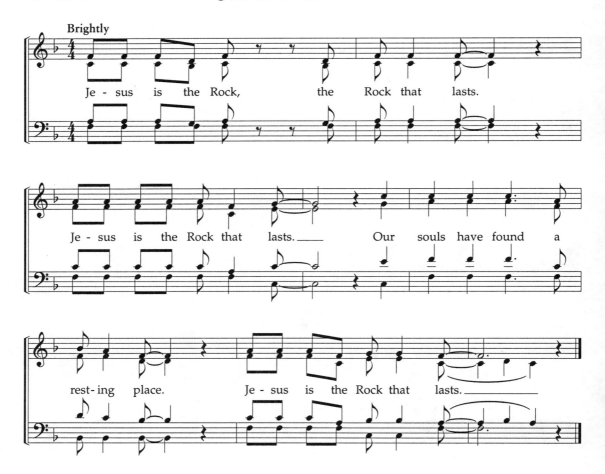

Individual names may be used in this song: "(Name) is on the Rock, the Rock that lasts. (Name) is on the Rock that lasts. (His/Her) soul has found a resting place. (Name) is on the Rock that lasts."

Words and Music: Ghanaian folk song, arr. Betty Carr Pulkingham

C-158 All the Riches of His Grace

(two-part song)

With simplicity

All the rich - es of his grace, all the full - ness of his bless - ing, all the sweet - ness of his love, he gives to you, he gives to me. me.

1. Oh, the blood of Je - sus, oh, the blood of Je - sus,
2. Oh, the word of Je - sus, oh, the word of Je - sus,
3. Oh, the love of Je - sus, oh, the love of Je - sus,

oh, the blood of Je - sus, it wash - es white as snow.
oh, the word of Je - sus, it cleans - es white as snow.
oh, the love of Je - sus, it makes his bo - dy

3. whole.   **Part II**
Oh, the blood of Je - sus,

Part I
All the rich - es of his grace, all the

oh, the blood of Je - sus, oh, the blood of

full - ness of his bless - ing, all the sweet - ness of his

Je - sus, it wash - es white as snow.

love, he gives to you, he gives to me.

This two-part song may be sung by men's and women's voices.

Words and Music: Jan Harrington and trad.
Copyright © 1975 CELEBRATION. All rights reserved.

C-159

Broken for Me

Refrain

Sustained

Bro-ken for me, _____ bro-ken for you, _____ the bo-dy of Je - sus _____ bro-ken for you.

last time

Verse 1

1. He of-fered his bo-dy; _____ he poured out his soul.

to Refrain

Je-sus was bro - ken _____ that we might be whole.

Verse 2

2. "Come to my ta - ble _____ and with me dine;

to Refrain

eat of my bread _____ and drink of my wine."

Verse 3

3. "This is my bo - dy _____ giv-en for you;

to Refrain

eat it re - mem - b'ring _____ I died for you."

Verse 4

4. "This is my blood _____ I shed for you,

to Refrain

for your for - give - ness _____ mak-ing you new."

last time

Slowly

_____ bro - ken for you. _____

Words: Janet Lunt
Music: Janet Lunt, arr. Mimi Farra

C-160

Coming to the Table

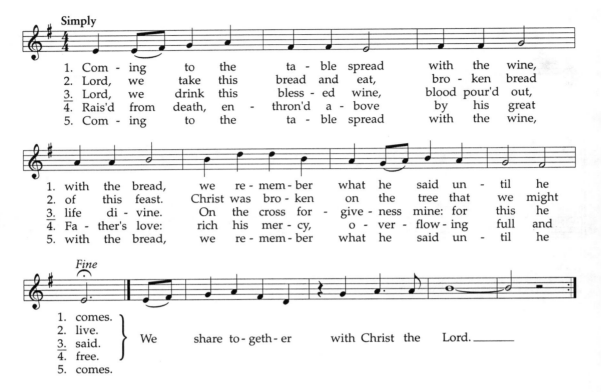

Simply

1. Com - ing to the ta - ble spread with the wine,
2. Lord, we take this bread and eat, bro - ken bread
3. Lord, we drink this bless - ed wine, blood pour'd out,
4. Rais'd from death, en - thron'd a - bove by his great
5. Com - ing to the ta - ble spread with the wine,

1. with the bread, we re - mem - ber what he said un - til he
2. of this feast. Christ was bro - ken on the tree that we might
3. life di - vine. On the cross for - give - ness mine: for this he
4. Fa - ther's love: rich his mer - cy, o - ver - flow - ing full and
5. with the bread, we re - mem - ber what he said un - til he

Fine

1. comes.
2. live.
3. said.
4. free.
5. comes.

We share to - geth - er with Christ the Lord.

Words and Music: Phillip Bailey

Jesus Is Our King

This majestic hymn is especially suitable as a postcommunion hymn.

Words: Howard Page-Clark and Sherrell Barker Prebble
Music: *Post Green*, Sherrell Barker Prebble

C-162 Now With God at Table We Sit Down*

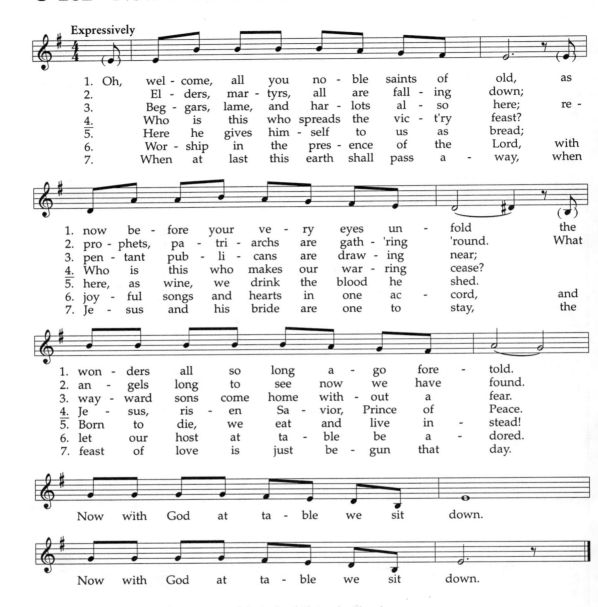

Expressively

1. Oh, wel-come, all you no-ble saints of old, as
2. El-ders, mar-tyrs, all are fall-ing down;
3. Beg-gars, lame, and har-lots al-so here; re-
4. Who is this who spreads the vic-t'ry feast?
5. Here he gives him-self to us as bread;
6. Wor-ship in the pres-ence of the Lord, with
7. When at last this earth shall pass a-way, when

1. now be-fore your ve-ry eyes un-fold the
2. pro-phets, pa-tri-archs are gath-'ring 'round. What
3. pen-tant pub-li-cans are draw-ing near;
4. Who is this who makes our war-ring cease?
5. here, as wine, we drink the blood he shed.
6. joy-ful songs and hearts in one ac-cord, and
7. Je-sus and his bride are one to stay, the

1. won-ders all so long a-go fore-told.
2. an-gels long to see now we have found.
3. way-ward sons come home with-out a fear.
4. Je-sus, ris-en Sa-vior, Prince of Peace.
5. Born to die, we eat and live in-stead!
6. let our host at ta-ble be a-dored.
7. feast of love is just be-gun that day.

Now with God at ta-ble we sit down.

Now with God at ta-ble we sit down.

This hymn celebrates the inclusive nature of the Body of Christ, the Church.

* Originally *God and Man at Table Are Sat Down*

Please Break This Bread, Lord

Verses may be sung by a soloist.

Words and Music: Jodi Page-Clark

C-164

Take Our Bread

Refrain

Flowing

Take our bread, we ask you; take our hearts, we love you; take our lives, O Fa-ther; we are yours, _____ we are yours. _____

Verse 1

1. Yours as we stand at the ta - ble you set. Yours as we eat the bread our hearts can't for - get. _____ We are the sign of your life with us

to Refrain

yet; we are yours, _____ we are yours. _____

Verse 2

2. Your ho - ly peo - ple stand - ing washed in your blood, Spi - rit - filled yet hun - gry, we a - wait your food. _____ We are poor but we've brought our - selves _____ the best we

to Refrain

could; we are yours, _____ we are yours. _____

This Is the Feast

C-165

Based on verses from Revelation, this hymn is especially suitable during Easter.

Words: Revelation 5:12-13, adapted, John W. Arthur
Music: *Ylvisaker*, John Ylvisaker, arr. Betty Carr Pulkingham

C-166

We Are Coming, Lord

Refrain
With confidence

We are com-ing, Lord,_____ to your ta - ble._____ We are
com - ing_____ to eat and drink to re-mem-ber you._____

Verse 1

1. We come as one bo-dy, u - ni-ted in your Spi-rit, bro-thers, sis-ters,
to Refrain
young and old, to cel-e-brate your life for us._____

Verse 2

2. We come, though un - wor-thy, to gath - er up the crumbs; yet
to Refrain
healed, re-stored, for - giv - en, through Je-sus, who died for us._____

Verse 3

3. We come re - joic-ing, with hearts for ev - er prais-ing, and
to Refrain
lips that are sing - ing of Je-sus, who lives in us._____

This song is useful as an offertory when Communion is to follow; verses may be sung by a choir or soloist.

Words and Music: Kathy Wood Thompson

Glorify Your Name

C-168   Jesus

1. Je - sus, _____ Je - sus, _____
2. Spi - rit, _____ sweet Spi - rit, _____
3. Fa - ther, _____ oh, Fa - ther, _____
4. Ho - ly, _____ ho - ly, _____

Je - - - - sus. _____
fill my _____ heart. _____
take my _____ heart. _____
ho - - - - ly. _____

Other verses may be added: "Hosanna..." "Worthy..." "We love you..."

Words and Music: Wiley Beveridge
Copyright © 1974, 1982 CELEBRATION. All rights reserved.

C-169   Sing Praise to the Lord for Ever
(two-part song)

Refrain
Brisk and bold

Part I
Sing praise to the Lord for ev-er and ev - er.

Part II
Sing praise to the Lord for

Call un-to him for hope in sal-va - tion.

ev - er and ev - er. Call un-to him for

Sing praise, al-le-lu-ia, sing

hope in sal-va - tion. Sing praise, al-le-lu-ia, sing

This two-part song may be sung antiphonally by two sides of the congregation or by men and women. Hand actions may be devised to portray the text.

Words: Jacob Krieger, alt.
Music: *Jacob's Song*, Jacob Krieger, adapted by Mikel Kennedy

C-170 Sing to our Father

Verse 1
Light and rhythmic

1. Sing to our Fa-ther, Cre-a-tor and King, who sent his Son, Je-sus, to suf-fer and bring us in-to his fam-'ly, oh, mag-ni-fy him.

to Refrain

Sing, sing, sing, sing, sing to the Lord of love!

Refrain

Al-le-lu-ia, al-le-lu-ia, al-le-lu-ia, al-le-lu-ia!

Verse 2

2. Sing to our bro-ther who of him-self poured out life to his peo-ple to see them re-stored. Sing to our hea-ler and sing to our Lord.

to Refrain

Sing, sing, sing, sing, sing to the Lord of life!

Verse 3

3. Sing to the Spi-rit; let us all hear and know that he frees us from sin and from fear to love one an-oth-er, to serve and to care.

to Refrain

Sing, sing, sing, sing, sing to the Lord of peace!

Finger cymbals and tambourine on the refrain of this song will enhance its "madrigal" quality.

Words: Stephen Ball and Jon Wilkes
Music: Lorna Ball
Copyright © 1977 CELEBRATION. All rights reserved.

Come into God's Presence

C-171

Smoothly

Come in-to God's pres-ence sing-ing, "Al-le-lu-ia, al-le-lu-ia, al-le-lu-ia."

Additional verses may be added: "Come into God's presence singing, 'Worthy the Lamb'..." "Come into God's presence singing, 'We love you so'..." "Come into God's presence singing, 'Glory to God'..." "Come into God's presence singing, 'Jesus is Lord'..."

Words and Music: anon., arr. Betty Carr Pulkingham
Arr. Copyright © 1975 CELEBRATION. All rights reserved.

C-172

Doxology

With movement

Praise God, from whom all bless - ings flow; praise him, all crea - tures here be - low; praise him a - bove, ye (praise him,) hea - ven-ly host: praise Fa - ther, Son, and Ho - ly Ghost.

This song is also appropriate as a grace before meals.

Give Him All the Glory

C-173

With sweeping dignity

1. Ho - ly, ho - ly, ho - ly is the Lord. _____ Ho - ly, ho - ly, ho - ly is the Lord.
2. Wor - thy, wor - thy, wor - thy is the Lord. _____ Wor - thy, wor - thy, wor - thy is the Lord.
3. Je - sus, Je - sus, Je - sus is the Lord. _____ Je - sus, Je - sus, Je - sus is the Lord.

Give him all the glo - ry, the glo - ry due his Name, glo - ry ev - er - more. Give him all the glo - ry, the glo - ry.

Ho - ly is the Lord. _____
Wor - thy is the Lord. _____
Je - sus is the Lord. _____

C-174

I Will Sing, I Will Sing

Verses

With vitality

1. I will sing, I will sing a song ___ un-to the Lord. I will
2. We will come, we will come as one ___ be-fore the Lord. We will
3. If the Son, if the Son shall make ___ you ___ free, if the
4. In his Name, in his Name we have ___ the vic-to-ry. In his

sing, I will sing a song ___ un-to the Lord. I will
come, we will come as one ___ be-fore the Lord. We will
Son, if the Son shall make ___ you ___ free, if the
Name, in his Name we have ___ the vic-to-ry. In his

sing, I will sing a song ___ un-to the Lord. Al-le-
come, we will come as one ___ be-fore the Lord. Al-le-
Son, if the Son shall make ___ you ___ free, you
Name, in his Name we have ___ the vic-to-ry. Al-le-

lu - ia, glo - ry to the Lord.
lu - ia, glo - ry to the Lord.
shall be free ___ in - deed.
lu - ia, glo - ry to the Lord.

Refrain

Al - le-lu, al-le-lu-ia, glo - ry to the Lord. Al-le-

lu, al-le-lu-ia, glo - ry to the Lord. Al-le-lu, al-le-lu-ia, glo-

ry to the Lord. Al - le - lu - ia, glo - ry to the Lord.

This song may be sung accompanied with only bass guitar and rhythm instruments, including light handclaps.
Other verses may be added.

Words: Max Dyer
Music: *Pulkingham*, Max Dyer

In the Presence of Your People C-175

Well-accented

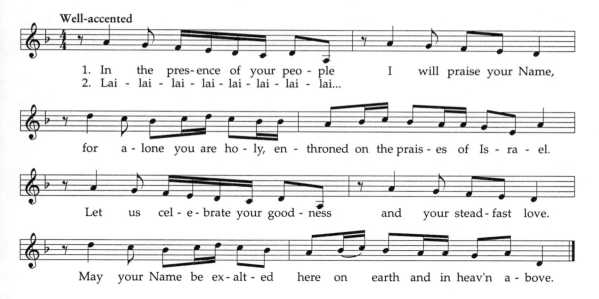

1. In the pres-ence of your peo - ple I will praise your Name,
2. Lai - lai - lai - lai - lai - lai - lai - lai...

for a - lone you are ho - ly, en - throned on the prais - es of Is - ra - el.

Let us cel - e - brate your good - ness and your stead - fast love.

May your Name be ex - alt - ed here on earth and in heav'n a - bove.

This song may be started at a leisurely speed and sung several times, gradually accelerating the tempo. A folk dance,
performed in a circle or line, can be devised to accompany this song.

Words and Music: Brent Chambers

C-176   Let Our Praise to You Be as Incense

An interpretive dance, using incense, would be appropriate with this song.

Words and Music: Brent Chambers
Copyright © 1979 SCRIPTURE IN SONG (a div. of Integrity Muisc). All rights reserved.

Make a Joyful Noise

Words and Music: Shirley Lewis Brown
Copyright © 1975 CELEBRATION. All rights reserved.

C-178 Oh, Give Praise to the King

Refrain

Brightly

Oh, give praise to the King, for he has brought you sal-

va-tion. So o-pen your heart and sing,

Fine

peo-ple of ev-'ry na - tion.

Verses

1. For his love, strong and true, his ten-der love pro-
2. From the dust hear him speak. He has___ come to

3. On the hill see him come, shin-ing as bright-ly
4. Come in joy, come in fear; know that the Lord is

1. tect-ing you, his faith - ful - ness to us is sure;
2. save the weak and raise them up to heights un - known,

3. as the sun, with hope and grace and power to heal.
4. al-ways near. His arm is might - y, strong to save

to Refrain

1. it will last for ev - er - more.
2. there to reign up - on his throne.

to Refrain

3. Wor - ship the Lord, be - fore him kneel.
4. from sin and dark - ness and the grave.

Words and Music: Phillip Bailey

Oh! How Good Is the Lord

C-179

Refrain *Joyfully*

Oh! Oh! Oh! How good is the Lord. Oh! Oh! Oh! How

good is the Lord. Oh! Oh! Oh! How good is the Lord. I

nev-er will for-get what he has done for me.

Verse

He gives us sal-va-tion, how good is the Lord. He

gives us sal-va-tion, how good is the Lord. He gives us sal-va-tion, how

to Refrain

good is the Lord. I nev-er will for-get what he has done for me.

Additional verses may be added to this song in thanksgiving for God's goodness to us: "He gives us his Spirit..."
"He gives us his blessing..." "He gives us each other..."

Words and Music: anon.

C-180

Psalm 8

Refrain
With joyful abandon

O Lord, our Lord, how great is your Name in the earth; O
Lord, our Lord, how great is your Name in the earth.

Verse 1

1. In the mouths of babes you es-tab-lish praise. Na-tions of the
to Refrain
world _____ end their war-ring days. _____

Verse 2

2. I see the heav'ns, the work of your hand; you placed the moon and
to Refrain
stars _____ ac-cord-ing to your plan. _____

Verse 3

3. What is man that you should care for him? You crown'd him with
to Refrain
glo-ry _____ and made him a king. _____

Verse 4

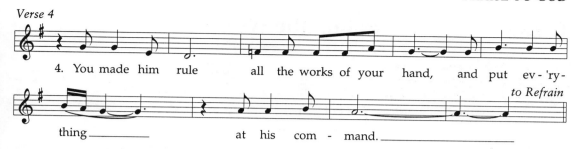

4. You made him rule all the works of your hand, and put ev-'ry-

to Refrain

thing_____ at his com - mand._____

Words: Psalm 8, adapted, Phil Higgs
Music: Phil Higgs

Psalm 148

C-181

Refrain

With rhythmic vigor

O praise the Name of the Lord our God; O praise the

Name of the King. O praise the Name of the Lord our God;

vss. 1, 2, & 3   *after vs. 4*

let all cre - a - tion sing.   a - tion sing.

Verses 1, 2, 3

1. Praise him sun and moon; praise him stars and light;
2. Praise him fire and rain; praise him storm and snow;
3. Praise him young and old; praise him beast and bird;

to Refrain

praise him in the earth; praise him in the height._____
praise him from the hill; let cre - a - tion know._____
crea - tures of the sea ful - fill his word._____

Verse 4

4. Praise him all you ru - lers be - low and a - bove;___

to Refrain

praise him all you na - tions, praise the God of love._____

Words: Psalm 148, adapted, Phil Higgs
Music: *Baylis*, Phil Higgs

C-182   Pullin' the Weeds

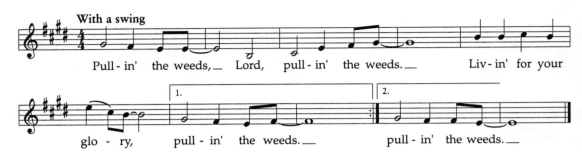

With a swing

Pull-in' the weeds, __ Lord, pull-in' the weeds. __ Liv-in' for your

1. glo - ry, pull-in' the weeds. __ 2. pull-in' the weeds. __

This simple song provides scope to celebrate the ordinary tasks of life, "the work God has given us to do". Verses should be improvised to suit the occasion: "Washing the dishes, Lord..." "Going to school, Lord..." "Singing a song, Lord..."

Words and Music: Max Dyer

C-183   Thank You, Lord

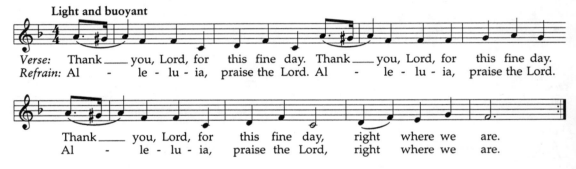

Light and buoyant

Verse: Thank __ you, Lord, for this fine day. Thank __ you, Lord, for this fine day.
Refrain: Al - le - lu - ia, praise the Lord. Al - le - lu - ia, praise the Lord.

Thank __ you, Lord, for this fine day, right where we are.
Al - le - lu - ia, praise the Lord, right where we are.

Additional verses, appropriate to the occasion, may be added: "Thank you, Lord, for songs to sing..." "Thank you, Lord, for our family..." "Thank you, Lord, for food to eat..." This song is suitable as a grace before meals.

Words: Diane Davis Andrew
Music: *Christian O'Connell*, Diane Davis Andrew

Thank You, Thank You, Jesus

C-184

This song of thanksgiving is appropriate after Communion.

Words: anon.
Music: anon., arr. Richard Gullen
Arr. Copyright © 1974, 1975 CELEBRATION. All rights reserved.

C-185   **The Butterfly Song**

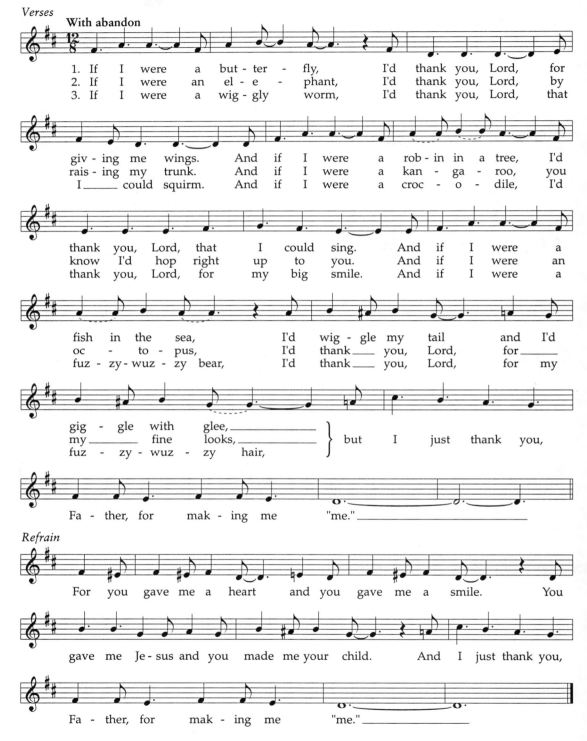

This song celebrates the joy of God's good creation, redeemable through his mercy and grace.

Words: Brian Howard
Music: *Live Oak*, Brian Howard

The Lord Is Present

C-186

Rhythmically

The Lord is pres-ent in his sanc-tu-ar-y, { let us praise the / let us sing to the / let us de-light in the / let us love the

Lord! The Lord is pres-ent in his peo-ple gath-ered here,

let us praise the Lord! Praise him, praise him!
let us sing to the Lord! Sing to him, sing to him!
let us de-light in the Lord! De-light in him, de-light in him!
let us love the Lord! Love him, love him!

Let us praise the Lord! Praise him, praise him!
Let us sing to the Lord! Sing to him, sing to him!
Let us de-light in the Lord! De-light in him, de-light in him!
Let us love the Lord! Love him, love him!

Let us praise Je - sus!
Let us sing to Je - sus!
Let us de-light in Je - sus!
Let us love Je - sus!

This song is suitable as an entrance hymn.

Words: Gail Cole
Music: *Church of the Messiah*, Gail Cole

C-187   We Want to Bless You

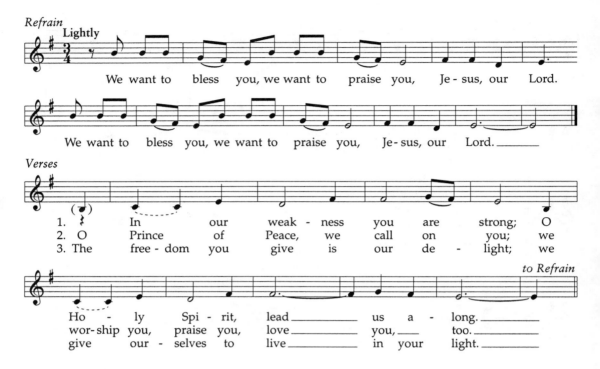

Refrain
Lightly

We want to bless you, we want to praise you, Je-sus, our Lord.

We want to bless you, we want to praise you, Je-sus, our Lord._____

Verses

1. In our weak - ness you are strong; O
2. O Prince of Peace, we call on you; we
3. The free-dom you give is our de - light; we

to Refrain

Ho - ly Spi - rit, lead_____ us a - long._____
wor-ship you, praise you, love_____ you,____ too._____
give our - selves to live_____ in your light._____

Allelu

Verses / **Lilting**

1. Come and bless, come and praise, come and praise the liv-ing God.
2. Come and seek, come and find, come and find the liv-ing God.
3. Come and hear, come and know, come and know the liv-ing God.
4. Come and bless, come and praise, come and praise the liv-ing God.

Verses for Christmastide
5. Come be-hold, come and see, come and see the new-born babe.
6. An-gel choirs sing a-bove, "Glo-ry to the Son of God."

1. Al-le-lu, al-le-lu,
2. Al-le-lu, al-le-lu,
3. Al-le-lu, al-le-lu,
4. Word of God: Word made flesh,
5. Al-le-lu, al-le-lu,

al-le-lu-ia, Je-sus Christ.

6. Shep-herd folk sing be-low, "Al-le-lu, Em-man-u-el."

Refrain / *Optional descant*

Al-le-lu, al-le-lu, al-le-lu-ia, Je-sus Christ. Al-

Al-le-lu, al-le-lu, al-le-lu-ia, Je-sus Christ.

le-lu, al-le-lu, al-le-lu-ia, Je-sus Christ.
(v.6 only) al-le-lu-ia, Em-man-u-el.

Al-le-lu, al-le-lu, al-le-lu-ia, Je-sus Christ.
(v.6 only) al-le-lu, Em-man-u-el.

The descant may be sung by a few light voices or played by a flute or recorder.

Words: Mimi Farra
Music: *Northfield*, Mimi Farra

C-189 Bless the Holy Name of Jesus

Words: Edith McNeill
Music: Edith McNeill

Canticle of the Gift

C-190

Refrain

Boldly

O what a gift, what a won-der-ful gift! Who can tell the won-ders of the Lord?

Let us o-pen our eyes, our ears and our hearts; it is Christ the Lord, it is he!

Verses

1. In the still-ness of the night___ when the world___ was a-sleep___ the Al-
2. On the night be-fore he died___ it was Pass-o - ver night,___ and he
3. On the hill of Cal-va-ry___ the world___ held its breath___ for___
4. ⸮ Ear-ly on that morn-ing when the guards___ were___ sleep-ing,___
5. ⸮ Some day with the saints___ we will come be-fore our Fa-ther___ and

1. might-y___ Word___ leapt___ out.___ He came to Ma-ry,___
2. gath-ered his friends___ to - geth-er. He broke the bread,___
3. there for the world___ to___ see,___ God gave his Son, his___
4. back to___ life___ came___ he!___ He con-quered death,___
5. then we will shout and dance and sing,___ for in our midst for our

1. he came to us,___ Christ___ came to the land of Gal-i-lee.
2. he blessed the wine; it was the gift of his love___ and his life.
3. ve-ry own Son___ for the love of___ you___ and___ me.
4. he con-quered sin,___ but the vic-t'ry he gave to you and me!
5. eyes___ to see___ will be Christ our___ Lord___ and our King.

to Refrain

Christ our Lord and our King!

This ballad recounts the life of Christ. The verses may be sung by a soloist.

C-191   **Glorious Son of God**

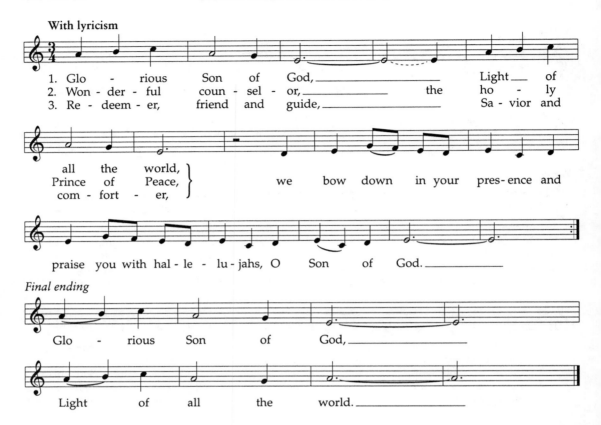

With lyricism

1. Glo - rious Son of God,_____ Light__ of
2. Won - der - ful coun - sel - or,_____ the ho - ly
3. Re - deem - er, friend and guide,_____ Sa - vior and

all the world, ⎫
Prince of Peace, ⎬ we bow down in your pres - ence and
com - fort - er, ⎭

praise you with hal - le - lu - jahs, O Son of God._____

Final ending

Glo - rious Son of God,_____

Light of all the world._____

This song is appropriate to the Christmas season.

Words and Music: David Burden
Copyright © 1981 David Burden. All rights reserved.

Hallelujah, My Father

C-192

With quiet devotion

Hal - le - lu - jah, my Fa - ther, for giv-ing us your Son,

send - ing him in - to the world to be giv-en up for all,

know-ing we would bruise him and smite him from the earth.

Hal - le - lu - jah, my Fa - ther, in his death is my birth.

Hal - le - lu - jah, my Fa - ther, in his life is my life._____

This song is most effective when sung in parts, accompanied with a few light percussion instruments: bongos, conga drums, claves, light handclaps.

Words and Music: Tim Cullen

C-193 **Hymn of Glory**

Refrain
With pulsing rhythm

Glo - ry, hal-le - lu - jah!

Glo - ry, hal-le - lu - jah!

Verse 1

1. Give thanks to our God and let him be praised with sanc - ti - fied hearts and hands that are raised.

to Refrain

Come join a song of praise to our God.

Verse 2

2. His Word ev - er true, the Son of his love, sing all the earth, to the hea - vens a - bove.

to Refrain

Hon - or and glo - ry be - long to our God.

Verse 3

3. Wor - thy the Lamb who was slain for our sins. He

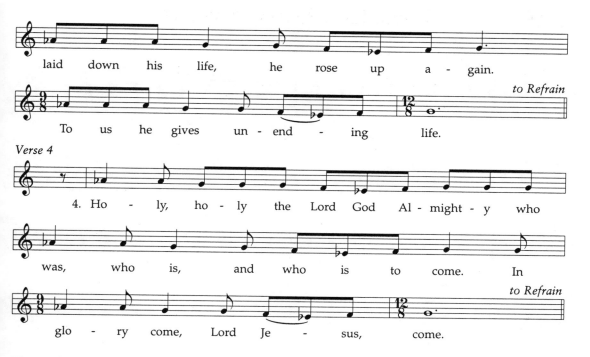

laid down his life, he rose up a - gain.

to Refrain

To us he gives un - end - ing life.

Verse 4

4. Ho - ly, ho - ly the Lord God Al - might - y who

was, who is, and who is to come. In

to Refrain

glo - ry come, Lord Je - sus, come.

The use of light bells will enhance the refrain of this song.

Words and Music: Charles Christmas
Copyright © 1974 THE WORD OF GOD MUSIC (BMI). All rights reserved.

¡Jesucristo Reina, Ya!   C-194

With bravura

1. ¡Je - su - cris - to rei - na, rei - na, ya! ¡Je - su - cris - to rei - na, rei - na,

ya! ¡Je - su - cris - to rei - na, rei - na, ya! ¡Al - le - lu - ya, a -

mén! ¡Al - le - lu - ya, a - mén! ¡Al - le - lu - ya, a - mén!

2. ¡Jesucristo sana, sana, ya! (Jesus Christ heals.)
3. ¡Jesucristo ama, ama, ya! (Jesus Christ loves.)
4. ¡Jesucristo viene, viene, ya! (Jesus Christ lives.)
5. ¡Jesucristo salva, salva, ya! (Jesus Christ saves.)

"¡Jesucristo reina, ya!" is Spanish for "Jesus Christ reigns!"

Words and Music: anon.

C-195 **Jesus, How Lovely You Are**

Softly, with movement

Je - sus, how love-ly you are. You are so gen - tle, so

pure and kind. You___ shine like the morn - ing star.

Je - sus, how love - ly you are. Hal - le - lu - jah!

Je - sus is my Lord and King. (my Lord and King.) Hal - le - lu - jah!

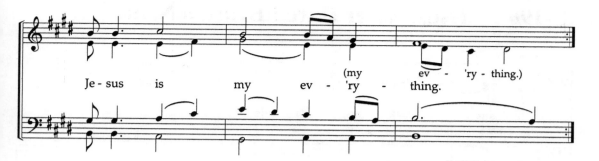

Je - sus   is   my   ev - 'ry - thing.   (my   ev - 'ry - thing.)

This song is most effective when sung unaccompanied, in parts.

Words and Music: Dave Bolton

C-196 Jesus, Never Have I Heard a Name

Tenderly

Je - sus, Je - sus, Je - sus,

nev - er have I heard a name that thrills my soul like thine.

Je - sus, Je - sus, Je - sus,

oh, what match - less grace that links that pre - cious Name with mine.

This song may be sung unaccompanied.

Words and Music: anon., arr. Betty Carr Pulkingham

Jesus, You're a Wonder

C-197

Other verses may be added: "Jesus, you're the Savior..." "Jesus, you're the lover..."

Words and Music: anon., arr. Betty Carr Pulkingham

C-198   Jesus Is a Friend of Mine

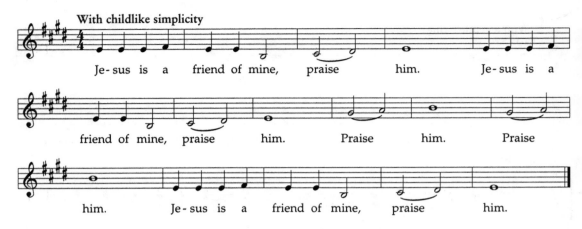

This song was written by a four-year-old child. Other verses are easily improvised: "Jesus loves each one of us..." "Jesus died to set us free..."

Words and Music: Paul Mazak, arr. Betty Carr Pulkingham

C-199   Jesus Is Lord, Alleluia
(two-part round)

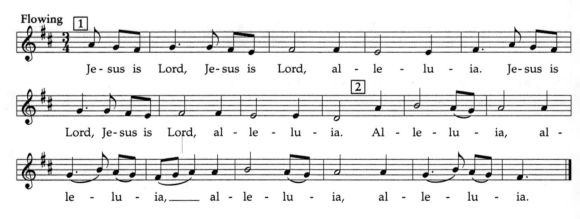

This song may be sung in unison the first time, beginning the round on the repeat.

Words and Music: Philip Moore

Oh, the Sweetness of Your Love

C-200

This "Gospel song" is especially appropriate during Easter.

Words and Music: Sandy Hardyman Stayner

C-201   Son of God

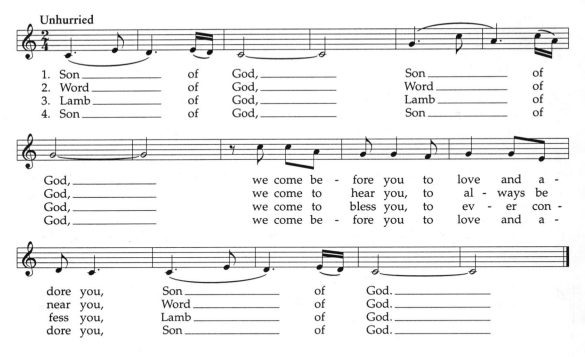

Unhurried

1. Son _____ of God, _____ Son _____ of
2. Word _____ of God, _____ Word _____ of
3. Lamb _____ of God, _____ Lamb _____ of
4. Son _____ of God, _____ Son _____ of

God, _____ we come be - fore you to love and a -
God, _____ we come to hear you, to al - ways be
God, _____ we come to bless you, to ev - er con -
God, _____ we come be - fore you to love and a -

dore you, Son _____ of God. _____
near you, Word _____ of God. _____
fess you, Lamb _____ of God. _____
dore you, Son _____ of God. _____

A flute or violin could introduce this lyrical melody.

Words and Music: Oressa Wise

C-202   There Is Power in the Blood

With an easy swing

There is power in the blood, there is power. _____ There is power

in the blood, there is power. _____ Je-sus, Je - sus, _____ Je - sus

Lord. _____ Je-sus, Je - sus, _____ Je - sus Lord. _____

Other verses may be added: "There is healing in his love..." "There is life in this place..." For Communion: "There is life in this bread..." "There is life in this wine..."

Words and Music: David McKeithen

Lord, Give Us Your Spirit

C-203

Refrain
Sustained

Lord, give us your Spi-rit, your Spi-rit that is love._____

Lord, fill us with your life, free-ly giv-en for the world._____

Verses

1. Where chil-dren cry let us wipe their tears____ a - way, and
2. Where there is pain let us be your heal - ing hands, and
3. Where peo-ple hate let us dwell a - mong them with love, and

to Refrain

where chil - dren fall let us raise them to their feet.
where there is grief let us com - fort with your love.
where peo - ple fight let us bind their deep - est wounds.

Verses of this song may be sung be a soloist or choir.

Words and Music: Sandy Hardyman Stayner

C-204   The Spirit of the Lord

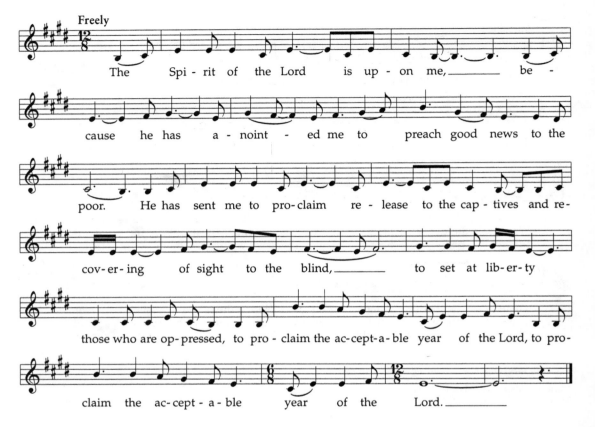

The Spi-rit of the Lord is up-on me,_____ be-
cause he has a-noint-ed me to preach good news to the
poor. He has sent me to pro-claim re-lease to the cap-tives and re-
cov-er-ing of sight to the blind,_____ to set at lib-er-ty
those who are op-pressed, to pro-claim the ac-cept-a-ble year of the Lord, to pro-
claim the ac-cept-a-ble year of the Lord._____

This song lends itself to "lining out," a technique where each musical phrase is sung by a soloist and then repeated by everyone. After it has been sung through in this manner, the entire song can be sung without the repeats.

Words: Isaiah 61:1-2
Music: *Good News*, Jim Strathdee, arr. Betty Carr Pulkingham

Wind, Wind

Refrain *Simply*

Wind, wind, blow on me; wind, wind, set me free; wind, wind, my Fa-ther sent the bless-ed Ho-ly Spi-rit.

Verse 1

1. Je-sus told us all a-bout you, how we could not live with-out you, *to Refrain*
with his blood the pow-er bought to help us live the life he taught.

Verse 2

2. When we're wea-ry you con-sole us; when we're lone-ly you en-fold us; *to Refrain*
when in dan-ger you up-hold us, bless-ed Ho-ly Spi-rit.

Verse 3

3. When un-to the Church you came, it was not in your own but *to Refrain*
Je-sus' Name. Je-sus Christ is still the same, he sends the Ho-ly Spi-rit.

Verse 4

4. Set us free to love each oth-er, set us free to live for oth-ers *to Refrain*
that the world the Son might see and Je-sus' Name ex-alt-ed be.

C-206   Blest Are All Who Fear the Lord

Words: Psalm 128, adapted, Phillip Bailey
Music: refrain, Ugandan folk song; verses, Phillip Bailey
Copyright © 1981 REDEEMER BAPTIST CHURCH, AUSTRALIA. All rights reserved.

Come, Lord Jesus

Refrain *Sustained*

Come,_____ Lord Je - sus, with heal - ing hands that bind us to - geth - er in u - ni - ty._____

Verse 1

1. Take from us our words that sound full of peace, but are on - ly sub - tle wea - pons to sep - a - rate us from each oth - er._____ *to Refrain*

Verse 2

2. Take from us our fear that keeps us bound, un - a - ble to reach out and com - fort one an - oth - er._____ *to Refrain*

Verse 3

3. Fill us with your Ho - ly Spi - rit. Cre - ate in us a new heart that reach - es out to hold each oth - er._____ *to Refrain*

Verses may be sung by a soloist or choir.

Words and Music: Diane Davis Andrew

C-208 Harvest of Righteousness

Verse 1 — Relaxed

1. He who sup-plies seed to the sow-er and bread for food will sup - ply, and

to Refrain

mul-ti-ply your re-sour-ces and in - crease the har-vest of___ right-eous-ness.

Refrain

Praise the Lord! Let the earth re - joice. Praise the Lord,_____ all ye_

___ lands! Praise the Lord! Let the earth re - joice. Praise the

Fine

Lord,_____ all ye_____ lands! (4. Pro -)

Verse 2

2. Of-fer-ing your ser-vice sup - plies the wants of the saints and pleas-es our God.

to Refrain

You will be en-riched in ev - 'ry way for your great gen-er - os-i-ty.

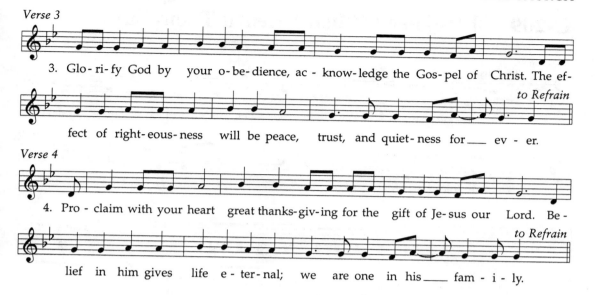

Verse 3

3. Glo-ri-fy God by your o-be-dience, ac-know-ledge the Gos-pel of Christ. The ef-

to Refrain

fect of right-eous-ness will be peace, trust, and quiet-ness for__ ev - er.

Verse 4

4. Pro - claim with your heart great thanks-giv-ing for the gift of Je-sus our Lord. Be-

to Refrain

lief in him gives life e-ter-nal; we are one in his__ fam - i - ly.

A simple folk dance, performed in a line or circle, can be devised to accompany this song of thanksgiving.

Words: 2 Corinthians 9:10-13; Isaiah 32:17, adapted, Bill and Margi Pulkingham
Music: Bill and Margi Pulkingham

C-209   I Rejoiced When I Heard Them Say

Words: Psalm 122, adapted, Betty Carr Pulkingham
Music: *Jerusalem*, Betty Carr Pulkingham

C-210

Let Us Give Thanks

Refrain — With vigor

Let us give thanks___ that our names are writ-ten,

let us give thanks___ that our names are writ-ten,

writ-ten in the book of life,___ in - scribed up-on his palms,

writ-ten in the book of life,___ in - scribed up-on his palms.

Verse 1

1. Re - joice not___ that dev - ils flee in his Name.

Re-joice not___ in the pow - er that he gave;

for he came___ to break the bonds of sin.

to Refrain

Yes, he did,___ he came to set us free, so free-ly we sing.

Verse 2

2. For he came___ to give us life,

that we might have___ it more a - bun-dant - ly;

came to break___ the pow'r of sin, he did.

to Refrain

Yes, he did, ___ he came to set us free, so free-ly we sing.

Verse 3

3. Let us give thanks, ___ thanks un-to the Fa - ther,

thanks un - to the Son, ___ thanks to the Ho - ly Spi -

to Refrain

rit, our Lord God, Three in One. ___

This song has particular appeal to youth.

Words and Music: Brian Howard

C-211 **Praise God for the Body**

Verse 1 and 4
Lyrical, unhurried

1. & 4. Praise God for the Bo - dy. Praise God for the Son.

to Refrain

Praise God for the life that binds our hearts in one.

Refrain

Joy is the food we share. Love is our home, Chris - tians.

Praise God for the Bo - dy. Sha - lom, sha - lom.

Verse 2

2. Guard your cir - cle, Christ - ians. Clasp your hand in hand.

to Refrain

Sa - tan can - not break the bond in which we stand.

Verse 3

3. Shed your ex - tra cloth - ing. Keep your bag - gage light.

to Refrain

Rough will be the bat - tle; long will be the fight, but:

This song is suitable for interpretive dance.

Words: Anne Ortlund, alt.
Music: *Love is Our Home*, Anne Ortlund, arr. Betty Carr Pulkingham

The Bell Song

With quiet joy

1. You got-ta have love _____ in your heart. _____
2. You got-ta have peace _____ on your mind. _____
3. You got-ta have joy _____ in your soul. _____
4. La la la la la _____ la la la (etc.)

You got-ta have love _____ in your heart. _____
You got-ta have peace _____ on your mind. _____
You got-ta have joy _____ in your soul. _____

You knew it was Je - sus _____ right from the start. _____
You knew it was Je - sus _____ there all the time. _____
The love _____ of Je - sus _____ will make you whole. _____

You got-ta have love _____ in your heart. _____
You got-ta have peace _____ on your mind. _____
You got-ta have joy _____ in your soul. _____

Final Ending

You got-ta have love _____ in your heart. _____

Small bells, keys, loose coins – anything that will ring or jingle – may be played on the "la, la, la" verse of this song.

Words and Music: David Lynch

C-213

The Celebration Song

Brisk and well-accented

1. For our life to-geth-er, we cel-e-brate. Life that

lasts for-ev-er, we cel-e-brate. For the joy and

for the sor-row, yes-ter-day, to-day,__ to-mor-row, we cel-e-brate.

For your great cre-a-tion, we

cel-e-brate. For our own sal-va-tion, we

cel-e-brate. For the sun and for the rain,

through the joy and through the pain, we cel-e-brate.

Ah!__ There's the cel-e-bra-tion!__ Ah!__

There's the cel-e-bra-tion!__ Ah!__ There's the cel-e-

bra-tion!__ Cel-e-brate__ the whole of it!

2. For his bo-dy bro-ken, we cel-e-brate. For the

word he's spo - ken, we cel - e - brate. For the feast - ing at his ta - ble, by his grace, ___ we are a - ble to cel - e - brate. For the Lord a - bove, ___ we cel - e - brate. For our Fa - ther of love, ___ we cel - e - brate. For the Son who is our bro - ther, for his Spi - rit, for the three to - geth - er, we cel - e - brate.

Ah! ___ There's the cel - e - bra - tion! ___

Ah! ___ There's the cel - e - bra - tion! ___

Ah! ___ There's the cel - e - bra - tion! ___

Ah! ___ There's the cel - e - bra - - - tion! ___

This song celebrates life in the Body of Christ.

Words: Jonathan Asprey, Tim Whipple
Music: *Celebration*, Jonathan Asprey, Tim Whipple

C-214

There Is a River

With abandon

There is a riv-er whose streams make glad the cit-y of God, the cit-y of God; the ho-ly hab-i-ta-tion of the Most High, the cit-y of God, the cit-y of God. God is in the midst of her, she shall not be moved; the Lord of hosts is with her. For there is a riv-er whose streams make glad the cit-y of God, the cit-y of God.

Words: Psalm 46:5-6, adapted, Jonathan Asprey
Music: Jonathan Asprey

Those Who Trust in the Lord
(two-part round)

C-215

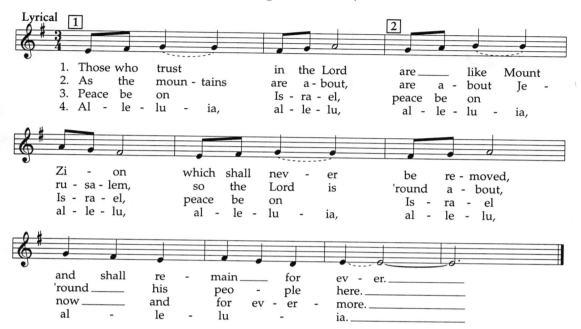

Lyrical

1. Those who trust in the Lord are___ like Mount
2. As the moun-tains are a-bout, are a-bout Je -
3. Peace be on Is - ra - el, peace be on
4. Al - le - lu - ia, al - le - lu, al - le - lu - ia,

Zi - on which shall nev - er be re - moved,
ru - sa - lem, so the Lord is 'round a - bout,
Is - ra - el, peace be on Is - ra - el
al - le - lu, al - le - lu - ia, al - le - lu,

and shall re - main___ for ev - er.___
'round___ his peo - ple here.___
now___ and for ev - er - more.___
al - le - lu - ia.___

Verses one, two, and three may be sung in unison, beginning the round on verse four. The entire song may then be repeated as a round.

Words: Psalm 125, adapted, John Smith
Music: John Smith

We Love the Lord

C-216

Quietly

We love the Lord, our neigh-bors and our - selves. We o - pen our
We love the Lord, who died on the cross.___ We love the

eyes, we see him ev - 'ry - where.
Lord to love each oth - er too. We o - pen our

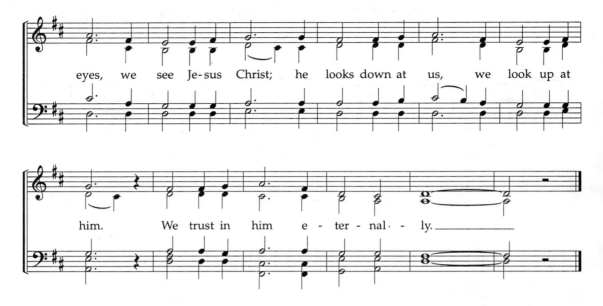

eyes, we see Je-sus Christ; he looks down at us, we look up at him. We trust in him e - ter - nal - ly.

This song was composed by a four-year-old child. Simple hand actions can be devised to portray the text. Sing in unison until the first repeat.

Words: David Pulkingham
Music: *The Old Smithy*, David Pulkingham

C-217   We Really Want to Thank You, Lord

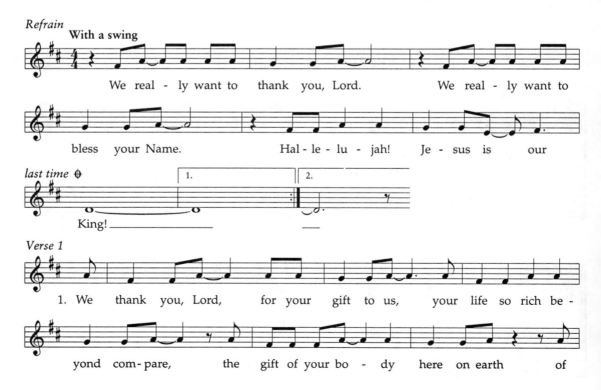

Refrain
With a swing

We real - ly want to thank you, Lord. We real - ly want to bless your Name. Hal - le - lu - jah! Je - sus is our King!

Verse 1

1. We thank you, Lord, for your gift to us, your life so rich be - yond com - pare, the gift of your bo - dy here on earth of

to Refrain

which we sing and share. _____

Verse 2

2. We thank you, Lord, for our life to-geth-er, to live and move with-

in your love, when we're set free with ten-der-ness to

to Refrain

serve you with our lives. _____

Verse 3

3. Praise God, from whom all bless-ings flow; praise him, all crea-tures

here be-low; praise him, a-bove ye hea-ven-ly host: praise

to Refrain

Fa-ther, Son, and Ho-ly Ghost. _____

last time

King! _____ Hal-le-lu-jah! Je-sus is our King! _____

This is a song of thanksgiving for life in the Body of Christ.

Words: Ed Baggett
Music: *The Way In*, Ed Baggett

C-218   Alleluia! Saints of God, Arise

Refrain
Triumphantly

Al - le - lu - ia, al - le - lu - ia! Al - le - lu - ia! Saints of

God, a - rise. Al - le - lu - ia, al - le - lu - ia!

Saints of God, a - rise and fol - low the Lord. ____

Verse 1

1. "Come and be clothed in my right - eous - ness;

to Refrain

come join the band who are called by my Name."

Verse 2

2. "Look at the world which is bound by sin;

to Refrain

walk in - to the midst of it pro - claim - ing my life."

This hymn of mission may be used as a dismissal song. Tambourine is effective on the refrain.

Words: Mimi Farra
Music: *Casa Merrill*, Mimi Farra

This page has been left blank
to avoid awkward page turns.

C-219   **You Are My Witnesses**

Refrain

Sturdily

You are my wit - ness-es   to the ends of the earth. ___

last time

You are my wit - ness-es   to the ends of the earth. ___

Verse 1

1. You are my peo - ple I love,   gen - tle as dove,

to Refrain

wise   and   harm - less ones.

Verse 2

2. You are my saints of new birth,   liv - ing on earth ___

to Refrain

___ but born from on high.

Verse 3

3. You are my pro - phets and priests,   pro - claim-ing my feasts,

to Refrain

tell - ing the won - ders of God.

Verse 4

4. You are my shep-herds of sheep, o - ver them keep - ing watch_____ by night.

to Refrain

Verse 5

5. You are be - lov - ed of God, liv - ing his word, dy - ing his death till he comes.

to Refrain

last time

wit-ness- es_____ to the ends of the earth._____

Verses may be sung alternately by men and women or by soloists.

Words: Betty Carr Pulkingham
Music: *Wargrave*, Betty Carr Pulkingham

C-220   **Children at Your Feet**

Refrain
Tenderly, well-accented

Here we are, Lord, chil-dren at your feet, _____

last time

_____ read-y to do your will. _____

Verse 1

1. Tell my peo-ple that I love them. _____ Tell my peo-ple

that I care, _____ for my peace is for them to

to Refrain

of - fer, _____ for my peace is for them to share. _____

Verse 2

2. Tell my peo-ple to share to - geth - er _____ all of their

wealth and pain; _____ for my Spi-rit is not one of

to Refrain

greed; _____ for my Spi-rit is not one of shame. _____

Verse 3

3. Tell my peo-ple that I lead them _____ as they so-journ

through this land; _____ for I walk this way be -

to Refrain

fore them; _____ for I hold them by _____ the hand. _____

will,   just read-y to do your will,   just read-y to do your will.

His Love Lights Our Path

C-221

Verses

With movement

1. Those who go out in weep - ing shall re - turn
2. Bless - ed be those who hun - ger; bless - ed be
3. Bless - ed are the pure for they shall see

in joy; the Lord is the source of our
those who thirst; God's right-eous-ness flows like a
our God and bless - ed are those who are

strength and peace, for God gives us rest,
might - y stream, and they shall be filled,
meek, for theirs is the earth,

for God gives us rest.
and they shall be filled.
for theirs is the earth.

Refrain

Then in joy
Then in strength } go we forth to pro - claim his
Then in pow'r

king - dom come! The Lord is our light and sal -

va - tion; his love lights our path,

his love lights our path.

C-222

Only Be Strong

Refrain *Boldly*

On-ly be strong____ and of good cour - age,___ be not fright - ened, nei - ther be dis - mayed; for the Lord your God ___ ___ is with you___ wher - ev - er you may go. ___

Verse 1

1. "Oh, _____ my chil - dren, ___ did you hear of the part-ing sea? _____ Do you know that I watch my *to Refrain* peo - ple ___ wher - ev - er they may be?"

Verse 2

2. "Oh, _____ my chil - dren, ___ do you know what I can see? _____ I can see the hun - ger *to Refrain* in your hearts ___ to be a part of my fam - i - ly."

Verse 3

3. "Oh, _____ my chil - dren, ___ I have called you, do you hear? _____ I have cho - sen you___ as my

to Refrain

wit - ness - es, _____ and there is noth-ing that you must fear."

Verse 4

4. "Oh, _____ my chil - dren, _____ e - ven though you

may not see, _____ I've pre - pared a place _____ to re -

to Refrain

ceive you; _____ just set your hearts now and fol - low me."

Verses of this song of encouragement may be sung by a soloist or choir.

Words: Jodi Page-Clark, based on Joshua 1
Music: Jodi Page-Clark

C-223   The Servant Song

With warmth

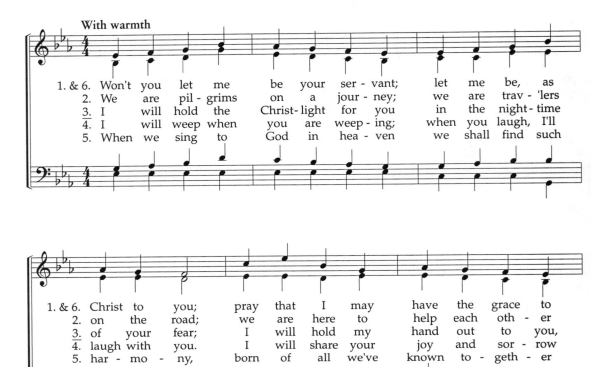

1. & 6. Won't you let me be your ser - vant; let me be, as
2. We are pil - grims on a jour - ney; we are trav - 'lers
3. I will hold the Christ-light for you in the night-time
4. I will weep when you are weep - ing; when you laugh, I'll
5. When we sing to God in hea - ven we shall find such

1. & 6. Christ to you; pray that I may have the grace to
2. on the road; we are here to help each oth - er
3. of your fear; I will hold my hand out to you,
4. laugh with you. I will share your joy and sor - row
5. har - mo - ny, born of all we've known to - geth - er

1. & 6. let you be my ser - vant, too.
2. walk the mile and bear____ the load.
3. speak the peace you long____ to hear.
4. 'til we've seen this jour - ney through.
5. of Christ's love and ag - o - ny.

Words: Richard Gillard
Music: Richard Gillard, arr. Betty Carr Pulkingham

C-224 God, Make Us Your Family

Refrain
With pulsing rhythm

Your king-dom come, your will be done, now that we are your daugh-ters and sons. Let the prayer of our hearts dai - ly be: God, make us your fam - i - ly. God, make us your fam - i - ly.

Verse 1

1. The eyes of the blind will be o-pened; the ears of the deaf will hear. The chains of the lame will be bro-ken; streams will flow in to deserts of fear.

to Refrain

Verse 2

2. The ran-somed of the Lord will re - turn; the is-lands will sing God's song at last. The chaff from the wheat will be burned; God's king-dom on earth, it will

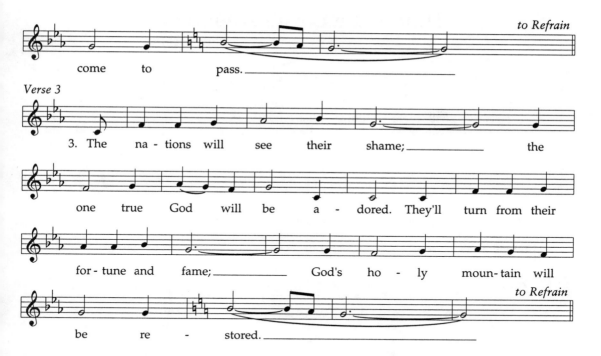

to Refrain

come to pass.

Verse 3

3. The na - tions will see their shame; the

one true God will be a - dored. They'll turn from their

for - tune and fame; God's ho - ly moun - tain will

to Refrain

be re - stored.

Words: Isaiah 35:5-6, 10, adapted, Tim Whipple
Music: Tim Whipple

C-225   Hail to the Lord's Anointed

This contemporary hymn setting is appropriate to Advent, Epiphany, and the Feast of Christ the King.

Words: James Montgomery
Music: *Yeldall*, Betty Carr Pulkingham

We Have Another World in View

C-226

This is a "marching song" for God's pilgrim people.

Words and Music: Ghanaian folk song, arr. Betty Carr Pulkingham
Arr. Copyright © 1989 CELEBRATION. All rights reserved.

C-227 We Will Sing to the Lord Our God

Refrain — With rhythmic drive

We will sing to the Lord our God, _____ might-y and splen-did is he!_

_____ We will sing to our Sa-vior and King, _____

last time glo-ri-ous in maj - es - ty. _____

Verse 1

1. Here is the Lord; he is a-mong us. _____

Let us wor-ship him to-geth - er. _____

Here is the Lord; he is a-mong us. _____

to Refrain
Let us praise him all to-geth - er. _____

Verse 2

2. Here is the Lord; let us walk with him. _____

He will lead and guide us through his land. _____

Here is the Lord; let us walk with him. _____

to Refrain
We will walk in peace through-out _____ his land. _____

last time

glo - ri - ous in maj - es - ty, _____ glo - ri - ous in maj - es - ty. _____

This song has particular appeal to youth.

Words and Music: Richard Gullen

Teach Us to Love Your Word, Lord   C-228

Refrain

Tenderly, with breadth

Teach us to love your word, Lord; _____ let it cleanse us through and through. _____ As we o - pen our hearts to o - bey you, _____ break us, re - make us a - new. _____

Verses

1. Your peo - ple were slaves _____ in E - gypt; _____ your might - y word set them free. _____ Call - ing them in - to a new land, _____ you led them safe through the sea. _____
2. When we were yet not a peo - ple, _____ your word gath - ered us in. _____ You made of us a new na - tion _____ to praise you in won - der and love. _____
3. Teach us to walk in your way, Lord. _____ Your kind - ness to us sets us free, _____ turns us to love one an - oth - er, _____ shar - ing your mer - cy and peace. _____

to Refrain

The refrain of this song may be used without the verses.

Words: Jodi Page-Clark, Martha Barker
Music: Jodi Page-Clark

COPYRIGHT ACKNOWLEDGMENTS

INDEX OF AUTHORS, SOURCES, AND TRANSLATORS

INDEX OF COMPOSERS, ARRANGERS, AND SOURCES

INDEX OF TITLES AND FIRST LINES

The first line of a song is included, in italic type, only where it differs from the title.